To
Mac
for
Mac

GW00734149

976

ALCOHOL DEPENDENCE

Postgraduate Psychiatry Series
under the General Editorship of
Professor W. Linford Rees
M.D., F.R.C.P., F.R.C.Psych., D.P.M.

Professor of Psychiatry, University of London;
Physician in Charge of the Department of
Psychological Medicine, St. Bartholomew's
Hospital

ALCOHOL DEPENDENCE

Brian D. Hore
B.Sc. (Physiol.), M.B., B.S., M.R.C.P. (London),
M.R.C. Psych., M.Phil. (London).

Consultant Psychiatrist, University Hospital of South Manchester,
Withington Hospital; Consultant I/C Alcoholism Treatment Unit,
Kingswood Clinic, Prestwich Hospital, Manchester; Honorary
Consultant Psychiatrist, United Manchester Hospitals; Vice-Chairman,
Greater Manchester Council on Alcoholism; Tutor, Summer School on
Alcoholism (Alcohol Education Centre)

BUTTERWORTHS
London   and   Boston
Sydney - Wellington - Durban - Toronto

THE BUTTERWORTH GROUP

ENGLAND

Butterworth & Co (Publishers) Ltd
London: 88 Kingsway, WC2B 6AB

AUSTRALIA

Butterworths Pty Ltd
Sydney: 586 Pacific Highway,
Chatswood, NSW 2067
Also at Melbourne, Brisbane, Adelaide
and Perth

SOUTH AFRICA

Butterworth & Co (South Africa) (Pty) Ltd
Durban: 152–154 Gale Street

NEW ZEALAND

Butterworth of New Zealand Ltd
Wellington: 26–28 Waring Taylor Street, 1

CANADA

Butterworth & Co (Canada) Ltd
Toronto: 2265 Midland Avenue,
Scarborough, Ontario, M1P 4S1

USA

Butterworth (Publishers) Inc.,
Boston: 19 Cummings Park, Woburn,
Mass. 01801

First published 1976
© Butterworth & Co (Publishers) Ltd 1976

ISBN 0 407 00082 8

Library of Congress Cataloging in Publication Data

Hore, Brian D
Alcohol dependence.

(Postgraduate psychiatry series)
Bibliography: p.
Includes index.
1. Alcoholism. I. Title. II. Series.
[DNLM: 1. Alcoholism. WM274 H811a]
RC565.H67   616.8'61   76-23443
ISBN 0-407-00082-8

Printed in England by
Billing & Sons Guildford & London

This book is dedicated to three of my teachers:

Dr. David Davies (Maudsley Hospital)

Dr. Griffith Edwards (Addiction Research Unit,
Institute of Psychiatry)

Professor Neil Kessel (University of Manchester)

CONTENTS

FOREWORD

Alcohol dependence or alcoholism is a problem of major medical and social importance in the United Kingdom and in many other parts of the world.

Definitions of alcohol dependence vary and, consequently, so do estimates of prevalence. It has been estimated that there are at least half a million people in England and Wales alone with a serious drink problem, and the prevalence is probably higher in Scotland and Ireland.

Alcohol dependence not only damages the physical and mental health of the individual but also affects his family, his social relationships, his efficiency and his working capacity. A recent report by the Department of Health and Social Security reveals that admissions to hospitals for alcoholism and alcoholic psychosis increased between 1959 and 1973 from 2,000 to 11,500 in England and Wales. Similar increases apply to the other parts of the United Kingdom and indeed to many parts of the world. Alcoholism is now a major cause of admission to psychiatric and general hospitals.

For a number of reasons, the diagnosis of alcohol dependence is frequently missed. Diagnosis is of paramount importance in that effective measures can be taken to help the person before irreparable damage occurs. Dr. Hore acknowledges the great importance of diagnosis and describes in detail the clinical features of the predependent as well as the dependent phase. Aetiological factors—social, physical and psychological—are fully and critically discussed.

The social importance of alcohol dependence is attested by the chapters on prevalence and road traffic accidents and communal behaviour. Alcoholism frequently comes under the care of general physicians and medical morbidity associated with alcohol dependence is comprehensively described.

Finally, the management of the disorder is discussed including identification of patients and the role of the hospital and therapeutic hostel in the comprehensive care of alcoholism.

The book is essential reading for postgraduate trainees in psychiatry and will be an invaluable source of information for physicians, medical students, social workers, members of the legal profession, psychologists and others interested or involved in the increasing social and medical problems of alcoholism.

Reference:

Prevention and Health—Everybody's Business. Consultative Document by Health Departments of Great Britain and Northern Ireland, H. M. S. O. 1976 ISBN 0 11 320188 5.

PREFACE

The past decade has seen a considerable rise in interest in the problems of alcohol abuse. After a period of complacency following the Second World War, it is now generally agreed that alcoholism or alcohol dependence is a major health problem in Britain, and is the major drug problem in many parts of the world. Books on the subject have tended to be written either for the intelligent layman or in encyclopedic form for the professional. The aim of this volume is to present a brief, yet reasonably comprehensive modern review of the subject for the professional reader, particularly for the psychiatric resident. It is hoped, however, that the book will be of value to other medical personnel, especially physicians and general practitioners. In addition, social workers and probation officers may find it of value in their dealing with alcoholic clients.

The author is indebted to Dr. Griffith Edwards (Director, Addiction Research Unit, Institute of Psychiatry, London), Timothy Cook, Esq. (Director, Alcoholics Recovery Project, London) and Jim Orford, Esq. (Research Psychologist, Addiction Research Unit, Institute of Psychiatry, London) for their most helpful criticisms. He would also like to thank Mrs. Doonie Swales, Mrs. Janet Chesson, and Mrs. Nan Allen for their most helpful secretarial assistance and Dr. Charlotte Feinmann for proof reading. The final draft of the book is, however the responsibility of the author. This book has had a prolonged gestation period, and the patience of the staff of Butterworths is personally acknowledged. It is hoped that this book will clarify a complex subject, and encourage others to develop an interest in an important and fascinating topic.

B.D.H.

1

INTRODUCTION

Over the past thirty years an attempt has been made to understand in a scientific manner the behaviour of those people who continue drinking despite obvious medical and social harm to themselves. Such people may be called different names, for example alcoholics, alcohol addicts, problem drinkers, alcohol-dependent persons, etc. What constitute adequate and agreed definitions of these terms has been and remains a problem.

The commonest term used is that of *alcoholic*. An early, much-quoted definition of this term is that of the World Health Organization (W. H. O., 1952): 'Alcoholics are those excessive drinkers whose dependence on alcohol has attained such a degree that it shows a noticeable mental disturbance or interference with their bodily or mental health, their interpersonal relations and their smooth social and economic functions, or who show the prodromal signs of such development. They, therefore, require treatment.' Such a definition obviously has irrelevancies, such as the phrase 'they require treatment', and has the anomaly of including the prodromal features of a syndrome in the definition of the syndrome itself. However, there are more serious problems (e.g. Seeley, 1959). These include the term 'excessive drinker', which raises the question, excessive compared with whom? This must be a relative term for it means anyone whose drinking goes beyond the traditional customary or dietary limits of alcohol used by the community to which that person belongs. Further, there is the use of social rather than medical criteria as part of the definition with the recognized difficulty of quantifying such variables.

1

There are, however, advantages in such a definition. The most important is the use of the term 'dependence', which in relation to alcohol has been described by Edwards (1967). It implies a state in which drinking appears to have become a dominating necessity rather than a 'take it or leave it affair', suggesting alcoholism is comparable to such disorders as dependency on drugs such as heroin and amphetamines. Dependency disorders are those in which there is physical or psychological dependence on a drug and are described later (Chapter 6).

Suffice here to say that alcohol in this sense is a member of a group of drugs producing psychological and physical dependence; the evidence for the latter is described in Chapter 10. Keller (1972) has described the alcoholic in somewhat similar terms. He considers that the consistency of choice in starting to drink, and stopping, is absent in the alcoholic. He says that 'at some time under the impulsion of some cue or stimulus which may be well outside his conscious awareness he will drink'. The term *alcohol addict* was used by Jellinek (1952) to refer to subjects who were physically addicted or dependent on alcohol. Such subjects showed certain phenomena, including an abnormal drinking pattern ('loss of control and inability to abstain'), craving for alcohol, increased tolerance to alcohol and the presence of withdrawal symptoms on stopping drinking. According to Robinson (1972), alcoholism itself was defined in these terms but was later widened (Jellinek, 1960) to become 'any use of alcoholic beverages that causes any damage to the individual or society or both.' This definition, which really relates to harm experienced by drinking, in part resembles the W. H. O. definition quoted above.

These two themes of harm and addiction or dependence are linked in a recent definition by Davies (1973). Alcoholism is considered by him as 'the intermittent or continual ingestion of alcohol leading to dependency (addiction) or harm'. He also emphasizes that there may be people (as is the case for tobacco dependence) who have a controlled addiction and dependence of a psychological sort.

Jellinek described five species of alcoholism: *alpha*—representing a purely psychological continued dependence without loss of control or inability to abstain; *beta*—that form in which physical complications occur without either physical or psychological dependence; *gamma*—alcoholism in which there is acquired tissue tolerance, adaptive cell metabolism, physical dependence and loss of control; *delta*—alcoholism which shares the same first three features of gamma alcoholism with inability to abstain instead of loss of control; and *epsilon* alcoholism (dipsomania), which is periodic alcoholism. Only two of these, gamma and delta alcoholism, are diseases in the sense he accepted, that of pharmacological addiction. His classic monograph (Jellinek, 1960) was entitled *The disease concept of alcoholism*. This concept has been the subject of much debate (Hershon, 1972), and has recently been examined by Robinson (1972).

As emphasized already, Robinson points out that whilst alcoholism as a disease was initially confined to gamma and delta groups, it became broadened to include all those who fall into Jellinek's broader definition. He considers harmful consequences have arisen from this. Firstly, an alcoholic client may define himself in medical terms, which may not be the view necessarily of the medical profession and vice versa. Secondly, if alcoholism is defined in medical terms the patient is relieved of responsibility, and thirdly, 'the medical profession will be considered to have competence in an ever widening sphere of life'. Robinson's paper has been reviewed by others in the same journal ('Comment on "The Alcohologists' Addiction" ', 1972) and also by Glatt (1974). It would appear that some of these fears have been exaggerated. For example, it does not automatically follow that being 'sick' implies no responsibility in regaining health—cf. the diabetic's responsibility for recovery. The attitude of Alcoholics Anonymous is of interest here in relation to the alcoholic in that whilst they believe the alcoholic cannot stop drinking once he has started, the responsibility for the *first* drink is placed clearly on his shoulders.

Secondly, modern psychiatric practices, at least as regards management of such conditions as alcoholism, very much require a multidisciplinary team approach as is emphasized in this book (Chapters 13 and 14). Hershon (1972) has also reviewed the subject. He gives two characteristics which satisfy the demands of a theoretical disease model. These are:

1. A disease should seem to be related to an aetiologically-relevant underlying pathological process. Thus, pneumonia is due to a bacterial invasion of the lungs and the inflammatory tissue response.
2. The essential characteristic is that the person so afflicted cannot decide by will-power alone not to have that pathological process and consequent illness; he cannot will or wish it away.

He emphasizes that the essential problem is that of poorly-controlled drinking and considers that this drinking is not on these criteria a disease. He states, 'If drinking is indeed difficult to control, it may well be due to a process of learned relief, or avalanche of certain noxious stimuli including, no doubt, the withdrawal symptoms themselves.'

It can be seen throughout much of this discussion that there are two recurrent themes. The first is defining alcoholics as those who suffer harm from drinking and the second is defining alcoholics in terms of dependence (addiction), be this psychological or physical or both; this second definition emphasizes the difficulty or inconsistency of control of drinking.

In this text, alcohol dependence is seen in terms of both Edwards' and Jellinek's restricted definition described above, that is, as a progressive condition in which, in the early stages, drinking behaviour is governed by psychological and sociological factors followed later by a stage of physical dependence as evidenced by the presence of physiological withdrawal symptoms. This does not imply that all subjects in the early stage invariably progress to the later stage, not does it imply once this stage has been reached that the subject has no control, rather that he has weakening of the consistency of control.

REFERENCES

Davies, D. L. (1973). 'Implications for medical practice of an acceptable concept of Alcoholism.' In *Alcoholism—A medical profile. Proceedings 1st International Medical Conference on Alcoholism, London*. Ed. by N. Kessel, A. Hawker and H. Chalke. London; B. Edsall

'Comment on "The Alcohologists' Addiction".' (1972) (papers by Moore, R. A., Dewes, P. B., Dumont, M. P. and Room, R.). *Q. Jl Stud. Alcohol*, 33, 1043

Edwards, G. (1967). 'The meaning and treatment of alcohol dependence.' *Hosp. Med.* 2, 272

Glatt, M. M. (1974). 'Alcoholism.' *Br. J. Hosp. Med.* 11, 111

Hershon, H. (1972). 'The disease concept of alcoholism—A re-appraisal.' *Proceedings 30th International Congree on Alcoholism and Drug Dependende, Amsterdam.* Lausanne: International Council on Alcohol and Addictions

Jellinek, E. M. (1952). 'Phases of alcohol addiction.' *Q. Jl Stud. Alcohol* 13, 673

Jellinek, E. M. (1960). *'The disease concept of alcoholism'.* New Haven, Connecticut; College and University Press, in association with Hillhouse Press, New Brunswick, NJ

Keller, M. (1972). 'On the loss of control phenomena in alcoholism.' *Br. J. Addict.* 67, 153

Robinson, D. (1972). 'The Alcohologists' Addiction"—some inplications of having lost control on the disease concept.' *Q. Jl Stud. Alcohol* 33, 1028

Seeley, J. (1959). 'The W. H. O. definition of alcoholism.' *Q. Jl Stud. Alcohol* 20, 352

W. H. O. (1952). *Tech. Rep. Ser. Wld Hlth Org.* No. 48, Expert Committee on Mental Health, Alcohol Sub-Committee. 2nd Report

2

CLINICAL FEATURES

These can be divided into those of (a) the *pre-dependent* phase, where drinking behaviour is best understood as the result of a combination of psychological and social factors, and the *sequelae* of physical dependence are absent, and (b) the *dependent* phase proper with evidence of physical dependence. The term *dependence* has been examined in relation to alcohol by Edwards (1967). It implies a state where drinking appears to have become a dominating necessity and to have gone beyond a 'take it or leave it affair' and one that cannot, except with difficulty, be broken. Dependence on any drug can be physical, psychological or mixed. Drugs producing physical dependence, such as barbiturates, heroin or alcohol, do so in a manner in which the personality of the subject is of secondary importance to the pharmacological effect of the drug. Drugs differ in their speed of producing dependence; thus heroin dependence may take weeks, but alcohol usually takes years. It should be noted, however, that young patients aged about 18 are sometimes seen with physical dependence with a brief drinking history, that is, one of four or five years.

Other drugs have pharmacological properties which produce a desired effect in certain personalities: this psychological dependence is the result of an interaction, therefore, between pharmacological properties of the drug and the personality of the individual. An example would be amphetamine. The majority of drugs, including alcohol and barbiturates, produce a mixed pattern of early psychological dependence and later physical dependence.

THE PHASE BEFORE PHYSICAL DEPENDENCE

Drinking behaviour

Studies such as that of Ullman (1962) suggest that in Anglo-American culture, drinking for most people begins in their teens and is sanctioned by parental figures. Usually boys are permitted to drink at an earlier age than girls, to drink spirits earlier and to drink away from the home situation at an earlier date. Clearly in such 'normal' drinking behaviour the attitudes of parents and society are of crucial importance and these matters are discussed more fully later (see Chapter 3). Suffice here to note that in Britain we knew little until recently of normal drinking behaviour. Edwards, Chandler and Hensman (1972) have recently examined normal drinking practices in a district of south-east London for five areas ranging from late nineteenth century trust development for 'working' families to a post-war 'luxury' development using direct survey techniques and obtained an 89 per cent overall response rate. Interesting and important differences emerged between different groups, some expected, others perhaps more surprising. Thus males drank more heavily than females, and social class I and II males tended to be lighter drinkers than subjects in other classes whilst the reverse was true of social class I and II females. Jewish people were absent in the moderate and heavy drinkers category, whilst there was a significant tendency ($p > 0.05$) for Roman Catholic male subjects to be heavier drinkers than Church of England subjects. Scottish and Irish men and women combined were more frequently represented amongst the heavy-drinking categories than English or Welsh. Males who had heavy-drinking fathers and females who had heavy-drinking mothers were respectively more likely to be amongst the heavy drinkers. Middle class males were more likely to drink regularly but in smaller amounts and to drink at home than were working class males, whose pattern of drinking was mainly beer drinking at weekends and in large amounts. Extraversion but not neuroticism was associated with higher drinking. It should be noted that this study is pertinent to an area of London. It cannot be necessarily inferred that it is applicable to other areas of the country. Consumption varies in different areas of England and Wales; thus, in the north-west of England the average household (1973) spent £1·83 per week on alcohol compared with a national average of £1·06*.

In relation to society's attitudes to 'normal' drinking behaviour we must also realize that attitudes are not static and will possibly be altered by pressure from purveyors of alcohol. It seems for example that at the moment in Britain there is a considerable liberalization towards women drinking in public places compared with formerly. Further, advertising on cinema and television is directed towards encouraging drinking amongst young males, drinking being equated with virility and masculinity.

* *Manchester Evening News*, 26 September 1973.

With regard to the drinking behaviour of the potential physically-dependent subject, it is rarely possible clearly to differentiate this from normal drinking. In some surveys, such as that of Marconi *et al*. (1955), so-called criteria of abnormal drinking have had to be abandoned because of the drinking patterns of the 'normal population'. Drinking behaviour, even if of regular and persistently large amounts of alcohol, in itself can rarely do more than raise suspicions of a drinking problem. Rather than the amount of drink consumed it is much more important to understand the reasons behind drinking. Clearly if drinking is required for a person to cope with situations of life, in terms of offering a 'psychological crutch', or if drinking becomes surreptitious or the person ensures drink is always available and his life is becoming 'alcohol-centred', it is suggestive that the patient is becoming psychologically dependent on alcohol.

Problems from drinking behaviour at this stage

These are much more likely to be understood in social terms than purely in terms of physical or psychological disturbance. Evidence to support this from general practitioners is described in Chapter 13. Perhaps the earliest is likely to be marital disharmony. There are likely to be objections by the spouse of repeated time spent away from the home drinking, disapproval of episodes of intoxication, and so on. Even here, however, there is likely to be a 'covering up' process by the spouse. Jackson (1962) has described how these attitudes go through three stages. Firstly, there is a denial or unwillingness by the spouse seriously to examine the problem; secondly, a rejection begins, with the spouse taking the children 'under her wing' and developing a 'parallel life' away from the drinking partner. Later comes the final stage of psychological and ultimately physical rejection with consequent separation and divorce. Although these basic patterns are seen in clinical practice they are not always so clearly defined and it has to be admitted we still know relatively little of the attitudes of female partners to the drinking companion. Even less do we know of husbands' attitudes to their spouse with a drinking problem. Here drinking often seems more covert and is usually strenuously denied. Drink is frequently hidden away from the male spouse in a variety of places, such as in toilets, beneath mattresses and in outhouses, garden sheds, etc. This covert pattern may be the result of society's attitude to the drinking female. Marital difficulties may be worsened by sexual difficulties, particularly impotence or a refusal by one partner to accept intercourse.

Apart from marital difficulties, difficulties are likely to arise in the work situation, although these may remain hidden for many years, particularly in Britain. Those in certain occupations seem more at risk for alcohol dependence, including merchant seamen, people in the hotel or catering trade, sales representatives, and people in the 'drink industry', although whether such people become dependent as a result of such occupations or 'drift' into them because of the opportunity to drink it is difficult to be certain. Too much should not be made of this predisposition of certain occupations. Thus an examination of occupational status of clients attending a Council of Alcoholism reveals a whole range of occupations represented (Merseyside Council of Alcoholism, 1972). Out of 641 cases there were 6 doctors, 5 directors, 6 school-teachers, 7 shop owners, 10 ship's officers, 2 hoteliers, 13 clerks, 6 decorators, 7 sales representatives, 13 dockers, and 6 street vendors. Difficulties at work are likely to be insidious and may represent absenteeism of initially a minor nature or an impaired performance. It is surprising how rarely is this detected. Thus Edwards *et al.* (1967) in a study of clients attending Alcoholism Information Centres found 50 per cent were in employment of a full-time nature and of the total who were not unemployed at time of interview 49 per cent had been with their employer for more than two years. Of the 264 men on whom they had data, only 2 per cent stated that they had lost no time from work, and the average number of days lost during the year was 86. In relation to lateness for work and Monday morning absenteeism 22 per cent and 21 per cent respectively of the sample said that this had occurred more than twice a month in the previous year.

Little is known definitely of the cost alcoholism makes in industry. Perfect (1971) estimated that at least 255,000 alcoholics in various stages of addiction are in employment. In Britain detection would appear to be hampered by the general attitude of industry both on management and trade union sides. There appears on the one hand to be a reluctance to accept that a problem exists and on the other a reluctance to have a potential problem investigated as by a survey carried out in industry. Too often there seems to be nothing done in the early stages and then when the situation is clearly evident the person is sacked. Very few companies have the alcoholism rehabilitation programmes familiar in the U. S. A. and despite the increasing interest in the general problem of alcohol dependence as shown by Government, medical and social work professions, etc., there seems to have been little progress, if any, in relation to industry. This may, of course, reflect the differences in Health Care Systems in the two countries. Thus in the U. S. A., with *no* National Heath Service, it is more likely companies will provide their own health programmes for employees. Hughes (1971) has reported American data on important signs in industry. As noted by supervisors these were: leaving post temporarily, absenteeism for a half day or a day, unusual excuses for absence, lower quality of work and mood change after lunch.

Difficulties in relation to the law comprise a separate chapter (see Chapter 11). Clearly, frequently drunkenness offences are likely and the futility of rearresting such people has been emphasized by Pittman and Gordon (1958) and others. At the time of writing, detoxification centres to deal with the chronic drunken offender are being planned in Britain. The importance of alcohol in relation to road traffic accidents is also considered elsewhere (Chapter 9). Increasing financial difficulties arising from non-discretionary spending on alcoholic beverages are likely to occur. These may manifest themselves in rent arrears, debts, etc. However, because of the 'Welfare State net' in Britain and the provision of social security it is uncommon today compared with the Victorian period to see abject poverty arising from excessive consumption. A further difficulty is aggressive behaviour arising from intoxication. In one study (Hore and Wilkins, 1976), this was evident in 25 per cent of the sample of patients as identified by the general practitioner.

Physical symptoms

Features of the physical withdrawal syndrome are by definition absent at this stage but certain physical symptoms may appear. One of the earliest is that of memory disturbance and usually takes the form of inability to remember events of the night before—a period of high alcohol intake with a rapidly-rising blood alcohol level. Such memory disturbances (palimpsests) may occur in anyone but their occurrence as a regular phenomenon usually indicates dependence of at least a psychological type. Memory disturbances are described more fully later (Chapter 10). Gastric symptoms, particularly anorexia (with accompanying falling off in the amount of food consumed), nausea and retching but rarely vomiting, may arise from the effect of alcohol on the stomach producing an acute gastritis (see Chapter 8). Epileptic fits are rare at this stage but more commonly seen in the stage of physical dependence.

Mental symptoms in the form of anxiety, depression or an admixture are not uncommon. Indeed in a study in general practice (Hore and Wilkins, 1976) they occurred in 13 per cent of patients. Such symptoms may form the basis of a vicious circle; their presence may encourage drinking, the difficulties arising since drinking tend to lead to more anxiety and depression and further drinking. Symptoms of this type are much more likely to be present at this stage than the classical neuropsychiatric syndromes such as Korsakoff's psychosis, alcoholic dementia and alcoholic hallucinosis. Depression may lead to suicide attempts; in males there is a greatly increased risk of suicide compared with a normal population (see Chapter 10).

The patient's attitude to his drinking

This has been well described by Kessel and Walton (1965) and frequently persists, often for years, into the dependent phase proper. Despite the problems created by the drinking the patient may not agree with the views of relatives, friends, helping agencies, etc. that there is any problem. There appears to be the development of a 'paranoid' attitude in which all difficulties are projected on to others. Blame for the drinking is laid at the door of the wife, employer or any convenient scapegoat. This lack of willingness to agree, let alone 'accept' the seriousness of the situation remains a major difficulty of treatment.

THE PHASE OF PHYSICAL DEPENDENCE

Jellinek (1960) described four features of this stage; there was one of two patterns of abnormal drinking; craving; increased tolerance, and the presence of the features of a withdrawal syndrome.

Pattern of drinking

The commonest pattern described in the Anglo-American literature is of 'loss of control'—the inability to limit intake once drinking has begun. Jellinek (1960) considered this phenomenon to be evidence of a physical addictive process, and such a view has found support from Alcoholics Anonymous, who often liken alcohol dependence to diabetes mellitus in its being a condition with a definite (although as yet undiscovered) metabolic anomaly which prevents the subject from returning to normal drinking. Glatt has recently reaffirmed the importance of loss of control (Glatt, 1972) although not necessarily implying a physical cause for the phenomenon. Indeed in 'learning terms' loss of control is a likely occurrence and can possibly be explained in terms of an approach—avoidance conflict (Chapter 5). Loss of control is sometimes clearly defined by patients who can remember a time when they did not drink like this, perhaps even a short time previously. In the author's experience, however, it is *by no means always so clear-cut* and it is difficult not to feel that the patient is sometimes made to talk in these terms by his attendant. Indeed, some go so far as to say it is the doctor's expectation that the phenomenon will occur that leads to the patient behaving in this way.

Keller (1972) has written a thoughtful review of the subject. He states that evidence obtained in an institutional setting does not imply the phenomenon to be an invariable accompaniment following alcohol ingestion. He considers that 'the characteristic symptom in alcoholism is that an alcoholic cannot consistently choose whether he shall drink and if he drinks cannot consistently choose whether he shall stop'. In other words the alcoholic cannot be sure that once he begins drinking he will be able to stop. As Paredes *et al.* (1973) state, 'On occasions an alcoholic is able to drink without continuing to the point of drunkenness when he is not exposed to the cues or variables critical for him, such cues might be absent in some settings.'

Ludwig and Wikler (1974), discussing loss of control, state that 'all that loss of control connotes is the relative inability to regulate ethanol consumption'. Further, in commenting on the failure of alcoholics in experimental situations (allowed a free choice of drinking) to become intoxicated, they note that even these subjects stole drink to produce high levels of blood alcohol. They see normal drinking as drinking limited by 'interoceptive and exteroceptive cues', and alcoholism as a condition where there is a failure to respond to such feedback material and limit drinking.

It appears probable that few authors now see 'loss of control' as an all or nothing immediate phenomenon nor do they regard it as evidence of a physically-addictive process but see it in psychological terms. Loss of control when it does occur is likely to lead to social difficulties, particularly those following intoxication, including drunkenness, quarrels or drunken arrest. Medical complications are less likely. 'Inability to abstain' refers to the ability to control intake which is, however, regular—usually daily and of a large amount. Such a pattern is not likely to lead to social difficulties but in middle life may well present as a medical condition such as cirrhosis, fatty liver, peripheral neuropathy, or other disorders. Davies (1973) has suggested that there may be many people who drink in this way without difficulties arising and who remain undetected. Such a pattern would appear commoner in countries such as France and normal drinking customs in Britain and France may account for the fact that loss of control is more common in the former, and inability to abstain is commoner in the latter.

Drinking at unusual times

Usual drinking hours are culturally and often legally inclined. In Britain it is unusual, with the exception of a few occupational groups such as dockers or market porters, for drinking to occur at breakfast time or on arising—indeed at any time before the pubs open around midday. Thus people who regularly drink at these unusual times may well be physically dependent and drink at this hour to stave off withdrawal symptoms evident on rising. It has been emphasized that patients smelling of drink at a general practitioner's surgery are also likely to have a drink problem. It is unusual, perhaps because of 'respect' for the doctor, for a patient to drink before visiting the surgery. Its presence in the study by Wilkins (1974) of alcoholism in general practice was an important indicator of a drinking problem, as defined in a questionnaire.

Craving

This phenomenon has been disputed by some because of its lack of overt presence in hospitalized alcoholics. It was discussed theoretically at a symposium (W. H. O., 1955) in 1955. A recent subjective enquiry has been that of Hore (1974). Seven hundred and fifty members of A.A. and the Renaissance Group (an upper middle class group of recovered alcoholics treated by the late Dr. Lincoln Williams) were circulated with a thirty-page questionnaire of which one third dealt with craving phenomena and possible related variables. A response rate of 47 per cent was obtained. Clients were asked if they had craved in the last week (craving was defined as an intense desire to drink) and to describe it in their own words. One third of the respondents had experienced craving. Descriptions of craving fell into the following groups. Firstly, there were descriptions very much akin to anxiety, for example 'a feeling that the nerves and tendons in my arms and legs are in tension. There is a permanent knot in my intestine, my skin feels like bursting.' Secondly, other descriptions were closely similar to those of depression. Thus 'a heaviness of spirits, a mental depression, a sense of having little or nothing to look forward to'. Thirdly, descriptions were like those of obsessional thoughts, for example 'a total obsession, complete inability to think of anything else. It is the thing uppermost in my mind to the exclusion of all else.' Some patients described craving in terms of more than one of these descriptions.

The client population fell into craving and non-craving groups. In terms of the presence of recent physical dependence and presence of stigmata of alcoholism and recency of drinking the craving group were significantly ($p > 0.01$) more likely to have these present than the non-cravers. Although the response rate was low, which may have introduced an element of selection, it would suggest that craving does occur and is inversely related to length of time abstinent and directly related to physical dependence. The largest single type of description referred to that akin to anxiety (64 per cent of patients who had experienced craving in the last week). In these patients craving may represent a state of hyperarousal akin to other emotion states such as fear or anger, which may from previous learning experience that alcohol relieves such feelings be doubted as being true craving'. In a further group craving appeared synonymous with depression.

Ludwig and Stark (1974) in an *independent* study administered a drinking and craving questionnaire to 60 alcoholics. Seventy-eight per cent of the subjects admitted to having experienced craving. Craving was defined by these patients either in terms of *'desired effects'*, such as reduction of tension, or in terms of a *'need'* or *'desire'* (this was akin on descriptive terms to the 'obsessional'-type phenomena described above). Craving was considered by these authors to occur when the alcoholic was emotionally dysphoric and during stressful, unhappy situations. The authors considered that the susceptibility to craving most related to the degree and extent of prior withdrawal experience. The experience of craving was regarded as 'a conditioned cognitive label which alerts the alcoholic to emotional dysphoria and which permits him to direct his behaviour to a potential source of relief—namely the ingestion of alcohol'. The link between craving anxiety and depression described here received further confirmation in a study (Hore, 1971) in which subjective ratings of these symptoms were made in individual patients over a period of six months and highly significant correlations were found between the variables. Littman (1974), using an 'intensive design model' in which two patients' symptoms as recorded in their own words were assessed under stress (superimposed group therapy) and relaxation (relaxation training sessions), found that in one patient 'the relationship between anxiety and craving under stress and non-stress conditions seem to have been demonstrated . . . and the stress—anxiety—craving—paradigm seems to obtain under the conditions specified, i.e. in a hospital setting in forced social contact, in group therapy, etc.'. In relation to the second patient craving seemed to be most associated with what might be called somatic symptoms, such as hand tremor and shakes, and with external cues such as being in a situation where other people were drinking. The affective and mood symptoms showed quite different patterns of fluctuation over the course of the investigation. Littman considers this model to fit more into the 'withdrawal syndrome' model of Ludwig and Wikler outlined below.

Ludwig and Wikler (1974) have published an important conceptual paper. They consider craving is common if looked for but very dependent on environmental cues, hence its absence in institutional alcohol-free settings such as hospitals. They consider it to resemble 'feelings' expressed by narcotic addicts, heavy smokers and obese subjects. In opiate addiction they recount how withdrawal phenomena can be classically conditioned to stimuli such as physical environment, drug associates and certain emotional states. In animals opiate withdrawal features can be conditioned, and 'conditioned abstinence symptoms' can persist for many months after withdrawal of the opiate. Human opiate addicts also report that after being off opiates, return to an environment previously associated with addiction can lead to symptoms being experienced strongly suggestive of early withdrawal phenomena. The addict also reports a feeling under such circumstances of strong desire for the drug. This is the 'yen'.

In relation to alcohol, Ludwig and Wikler consider similar phenomena may exist. They see 'craving for alcohol comparable with craving for narcotics' as representing the psychological and cognitive correlate of a sub-clinical conditioned withdrawal syndrome. They go on to state that 'the more frequent and severe the prior withdrawal experiences the greater the predisposition to conditioned withdrawal symptoms with a consequent desire for relief, i.e. craving.' Such conditioning, they consider, could be brought about by 'exteroceptive' and 'interoceptive' stimuli. Interoceptive conditioning would arise from any cause producing psychological arousal resembling the alcohol withdrawal syndrome or ingestion of a drug which in a recovered alcoholic acts as a conditioned stimulus evoking conditioned withdrawal responses. In relation to exteroceptive conditioning, this would result in a conditioned withdrawal syndrome sub-clinical in nature with associated craving when an alcoholic is exposed to cues relevant to previous drinking situations.

These concepts, together with studies already described, suggest that craving is the cognitive label given by subjects to an internal state of either psychological arousal or a sub-clinical alcohol withdrawal syndrome. Such labelling directs the subject to goal-orientated behaviour to relieve that state, i.e. drinking.

Tolerance

In the early stages of physical dependence, increased tolerance, that is, the effect of more alcohol being required to produce the same effect, is frequently noted. This phenomenon of tolerance is well recognized in other forms of drug dependency. Later, tolerance may decline so that less alcohol produces the same effect.

Withdrawal symptoms

The alcohol withdrawal syndrome and its management is considered in detail in a later chapter (Chapter 10). The earliest phenomenon is the tremor, usually bilateral and most marked in the hands. This may cause a cup and saucer to be held unsteadily and this has been suggested as a useful diagnostic tool, particularly for the general practitioner (Lloyd, 1973). Such a tremor classically occurs in the morning when there has been a withdrawal period of several hours and is called the 'morning shakes'. It is often accompanied by autonomic phenomena such as sweating, malaise and nausea, and retching. Later, transient hallucinations of a visual or auditory nature may occur, as may fits which may be isolated phenomena or part of the fully-developed withdrawal syndrome, delirium tremens. This usually begins 48–72 hours after abstinence. Withdrawal of alcohol to produce these phenomena may not be absolute but relative, that is, a reduction in the amount of alcohol consumed. Often the full-blown syndrome is abated by the patient drinking early in the morning, as he soon learns that such drinking may stave off the symptoms. It is in situations where there is little likelihood of alcohol being available, such as a prison cell or hospital ward, that the full-blown syndrome may develop. It is not rare for alcohol dependence to be first diagnosed in a medical ward when a patient presents with delirium tremens.

The classic physical *sequelae* of excessive drinking, namely cirrhosis, peripheral neuropathy and cardiomyopathy, may still be absent and may require a further period of years to develop.

As physical dependence progresses, there is a gradual downward decline in overall function ending in a minority of cases in the 'Skid Row' figure (Edwards *et al.*, 1966). It is important to realize, however, that many people will not reach this stage. The danger lies in this group of people who are social derelicts becoming synonymous with alcoholic or alcohol-dependent subjects and the end state becoming the only form recognized.

Physical examination

In the pre-dependent phase this may be unrewarding. In the dependent phase, there may be evidence of tremor and memory impairment and possibly in both stages there may be features of physical disease, such as neuropathy, cirrhosis, cardiomyopathy, etc. These physical *sequelae* are considered in detail later.

The time scale in which alcohol dependence develops may be variable. The fact that most patients present in their forties may be coincidental. Many patients when seen first in hospital practice have shown features of physical dependence for some years and have been advised to seek help several years previously. A minority of patients present at a young age; approximately 15 per cent of in-patients at the Alcoholism Treatment Unit in Manchester are under 25 years of age, some even 17 or 18 years of age and with a history of only two or three years of drinking. Such patients frequently show signs of physical dependence.

REFERENCES

Davies, D. L. (1973). 'Implications for medical practice of an acceptable concept of alcoholism.' *Alcoholism: a medical profile. Proceedings 1st International Medical Conference on Alcoholism*, Ed. by N. Kessel A. Hawker and H. Chalke, London; B. Edsall

Edwards, G. (1967). 'The Meaning and Treatment of Alcohol Dependence.' *Hosp. Med.* **2**, 272

Edwards, G., Hawker, A., Williamson, V. and Hensman, C. (1966). 'London's Skid Row.' *Lancet* **1**, 249

Edwards, G., Fisher, M. K., Hawker, A. and Hensman, C. (1967). 'Clients of Alcoholism Information Centres. *Br. med. J.* **4**, 346

Edwards, G., Chandler, J. and Hensman, C. (1972). 'Drinking in a London suburb–I. 'Correllates of normal drinking.' *Q. Jl Stud. Alcohol* Supplement No. 6, p. 69

Glatt, M. M. (1972). 'The hazy borderline of the loss of control.' In *Proceedings 30th International Congress of Alcoholism and Drug Dependence, Amsterdam, 1972.* Lausanne; International Council on Alcohol and Addictions

Hore, B. D. (1971). 'Factors in alcoholic relapse.' *Br. J. Addict,* **66**, 89

Hore, B. D. (1974). 'Craving for alcohol.' *Br. J. Addict.* **69**, 13

Hore, B. D. and Wilkins, R. H. (1976). 'A general practitioner study of the commonest presenting symptoms of alcoholism. *J. R. Coll. gen. Practnrs* **26**, 140

Hughes, J. A. W. (1971). 'How can industry identify the alcoholic?' *Camberwell Council on Alcoholism Journal* **2**(4), 18. 101 Denmark Hill, London SE5

Jackson, J. K. (1962). 'Alcoholism and the family.' In *Society, culture and drinking patterns.* Ed. by D. J. Pittman and C. R. Snyder, New York; J. Wiley

Jellinek, E. M. (1960). *The disease concept of alcoholism.* New Haven, Connecticut; College and University Press, in association with Hillhouse Press, New Brunswick, NJ

Keller, M. (1972). 'On the loss of control phenomenon in alcoholism.' *Br. J. Addict.* **67**, 153

Kessel, N. and Walton, H. (1965). *Alcoholism.* London; Penguin.

Littman, G. (1974). Addiction Research Unit, Institute of Psychiatry, De Crespigny Park, London SE5

Lloyd, G. (1973). Personal communication.

Ludwig, A. M. and Wikler, A. (1974). 'Craving and relapse to drink.' *Q. Jl Stud. Alcohol* **35,** 108

Ludwig, A. M. and Stark, L. H. (1974). 'Alcohol Craving, Subjective and Situational Aspects.' *Q. Jl Stud. Alcohol* **35,** 899

Marconi, J., Varela, A., Rosenblat, E., Solari, G., Marchesse, I., Alvarado, R. and Enriques, W. (1955). 'A survey on the prevalence of alcoholism among the adult population of a suburb in Santiago.' *Q. Jl Stud. Alcohol* **16,** 438

Merseyside Council of Alcoholism (1972). Report. Merseyside Council Chambers B15, The Temple, Dale Street, Liverpool L2 5RU

Paredes, A., Hood, W. R., Seymour H. and Gollo, B. M. (1973). 'Loss of control in alcoholism.' *Q. Jl Stud. Alcohol* **34,** 1146

Perfect, P. (1971). 'The Alcoholic in Employment.' Publication of the National Council of Alcoholism, London

Pittman, D. J. and Gordon, C. W. (1958). 'Revolving door.' *A study of the chronic police court inebriate.* Glencoe, Illinois; The Free Press

Ullman, A. D. (1962). 'First drinking experience as related to age and sex.' In *Society, culture and drinking patterns.'* Ed. by D. J. Pittman and C. R. Snyder, New York; John Wiley

W. H. O. (1955). Symposium on 'The craving for alcohol.' *Q. Jl Stud. Alcohol* **16,** 34

Wilkins, R. H. (1974). *The hidden alcoholic in general practice.* London; Elek Science

3

AETIOLOGICAL FACTORS–
I. SOCIAL FACTORS

'In the U. S. A. there are 40,000,000 users of alcohol and 600,000 chronic alcoholics and the drinking habits of 39,400,000 normal drinkers would be the logical starting point of a fundamental study of the problem of alcohol.'

Horton (1943)

The importance of social factors in influencing dependency has been insufficiently known in Britain. Cultural factors in influencing drinking behaviour have rarely been studied by British sociologists, in contrast to the situation found in the U. S. A. The W. H. O. definition of alcoholism (1952) implied a pattern of drinking different to the cultural norm. The definition states that 'alcoholics are those excessive drinkers whose dependence on alcohol has attained such a degree it shows a noticeable mental disturbance or interference with their bodily or mental health, their interpersonal relations and their smooth social and economic functioning or who show prodromal signs of such development' (they therefore require treatment). Excessive drinkers raise the question, 'excessive compared with whom?' We are told it refers to those whose drinking goes beyond the traditional customary or dietary levels of alcohol used by the community in which they belong. Thus, even in discussing the definition of alcoholism we are immediately involved in drinking in relation to the cultural norm. Jellinek (1960) describes further how different communities identify different patterns of drinking as the prime 'drinking problem' in their community. He describes how in Finland the major drinking problems are those of workmen who come to cities every few weeks 'on the spree' and whose drinking is accompanied by aggressive behaviour. In Latin countries major problems may arise from 'fiesta drinking' whilst in France ill health may arise from regular persistent drinking without

18

overt signs of intoxication. In these countries such people may be called alcoholics, but this is not the common view in Britain of what is an alcoholic. Who is called an alcoholic may thus depend on the society the person lives in.

The differences between an alcoholic population and a non-alcoholic population in any culture can be explained in one of two ways. This dichotomy runs widely through other areas of social pathology such as crime, delinquency, drug addiction, etc. Firstly, there is the idea of individual propensity; that is, there is something uniquely different about the alcoholic or potential alcoholic in relation to his non-alcoholic peers. This difference may have a physical basis (genetic or acquired) or a psychological one, and this viewpoint is described below. Secondly, there is the view that prime importance lies not in individual differences but in the social environment in which the potential alcoholic develops. The view is well put by Ullman (1952), an American sociologist who in discussing the possible use of alcohol to relieve tension, states that 'everyone has problems of tension reduction; and that the differentia of alcoholism viewed as a mechanism of relief from tension are to be found *not* at the level of personality but rather in variations in the conditions in which drinking is learned, and in the availability of alternative patterns for relieving tension.'

Numerous epidemiological and sociological studies carried out over the last thirty years have shown how patterns of drinking and attitudes to drinking differ in different cultural groups. It has been clearly established that different ethnic groups exhibit different cultural attitudes to the use of alcohol and show different rates of drinking pathologies and alcoholism. For example, in the U. S. A. Jews, Chinese and Italians have low rates of alcoholism, in contrast to the Irish, who have high rates. The difference between the Jews and Irish is maintained in England (Edwards, Chandler and Hensman, 1972). Within the British Isles drinking pathologies seem higher in Scotland than in England. It is this realization that alcoholism prevalence rates differ in different ethnic groups often within the same country that has led to the realization that such differences cannot be wholly explained in terms of psychological or physical theories and are explicable at least in part by different attitudes to drinking within these ethnic groups.

Before considering drinking attitudes in Western society and their possible implication in the genesis of alcoholism, let us consider studies of non-Western cultures in which drinking behaviour is understood in terms of the structure of that society. The earliest comprehensive study was that of Horton (1943). Although an anthropologist, he was influenced by Dollard and Miller's view of the importance of anxiety in motivating human behaviour. In a study of the drinking patterns of 59 tribal societies he concluded that insobriety amongst males was significantly related to subsistence insecurity (anxiety) and to the degree of acculturation being undergone by that society (acculturation refers to the process of cultural exchange induced by contact with foreign cultures). Field (1962) carried out a later cross cultural study using the data from Horton's tribes and a small number of additional tribes. He also used different scales to assess drinking behaviour. He reached the different conclusion that the degree of drunkenness in a society was related to the degree of formal organization of that society. Societies firmly structured with lineal social solidarity, and having interpersonal relationships structured along hierarchical and respectful lines were the more sober ones. He considered drunkenness was independent of the level of anxiety in any society and that Horton's measures of an insecure food supply and acculturation were really measures of a loose social organization and this explained his correlations. His conclusion that drinking behaviour is influenced by the 'firmness' of the society is interesting in Western society in relation to the increased drinking by Jews when they move out of a strictly Jewish community into a Gentile one.

A study of drinking behaviour within a tribal society is that of Sangree (1962). Sangree studied the Bantu Tiriki in Kenya, and concluded that the manner in which an individual drank was a guide to his status in that society (see also Edwards, Chandler and Hensman, 1972). The importance of social factors in influencing drinking behaviour has been studied extensively in the U. S. A., particularly in relation to drinking practices amongst Jewish and Irish migrants. Various explanations have been put forward by sociologists to explain the marked differences in these ethnic groups in relation to drinking pathologies. One of the earliest and most comprehensive was that of Bales (1946). He considered there were three major ways in which culture and social organization influenced drinking pathology. Firstly, 'dynamic factors', which refer to the degree to which the culture operates to bring about acute needs for adjustment of inner tensions in its members, including guilt induced by the culture, and sexual tensions. Secondly, 'orientating factors', which are the sort of attitudes towards drinking which the culture induces in its members; most important is whether these attitudes approve of the individual solving tensions by drinking or whether they induce strong counter-anxiety towards drinking. Thirdly, 'alternative behaviour', referring to the degree to which the culture provides a suitable substitute means of satisfaction. Let us now consider these factors in relation to the Jewish and Irish cultures. In 1840 an Irish priest speaking of his fellow-countrymen said: 'In truth, not only were our countrymen remarkable for their intemperate use of intoxicating liquors but intemperance has already entered into and formed a part of the national character. An Irishman and a drunkard had become synonymous terms, wherever he was introduced in character in the theatre or on the pages of the novelist he should be represented habited in rags, bleeding at the nose, and waving a shillelagh. Whiskey was everywhere regarded as an idol.' Bales considered cultural factors which encouraged drinking amongst the Irish to include: dietary use of alcohol as a substitute for food, which was often difficult to obtain; absence of ritualistic drinking—drinking of alcohol was not invested with symbolic and ritualistic religious rites (compare the Jewish position outlined below); a tolerance of drinking by the Catholic church; drink being synonymous with hospitality and social functioning; rigid pre-marital separation of the sexes, and strong premarital sexual taboos encouraging young males to spend their spare time drinking with fellow men, which led to considerable suspiciousness of the male abstainer; non-disapproval of drunkenness by society; and finally, use of alcohol as a way of solving problems. In essence he considered the Irish has a *'convivial–ultilitarian'* attitude to drinking. The 'orientating' factors towards the use of drink amongst the Irish were thus strong. Bales's evidence for this viewpoint was from documentary sources relating to nineteenth century rural Ireland. Whether such views pertain to the Irish at present in the U. S. A., and indeed to the Irish in Ireland may seem doubtful. Indeed, O'Connor (*née* Fitzpatrick) considers, in a study of drinking practices amongst young people (personal communication, 1972), that the contemporary Irish have an ambivalent attitude to drinking: there are two value systems in relation to drinking operating in the culture which are directly opposed. It is of interest that today, whilst the rate of alcoholic admissions to mental hospitals in Eire remains high (resembling that in England at the turn of the century), Ireland is one of the few remaining countries to have a strong abstinence movement as exemplified by the Pioneer's Association. O'Connor also considers that in the Irish of the nineteenth century the abstinence movement was also evident and that this aspect of Irish society was ignored by Bales. Her view is that an ambivalent culture is likely to lead to a higher rate of drinking pathologies as the young are in a much more difficult position in relation to drinking behaviour than in those societies where clear guide-lines are given, as in Jewish communities.

Bales's view of the Jewish culture was that it had a 'ritualistic' use of alcohol as compared with the 'convivial–utilitarian' view of the Irish and this explained the fact that although Jews drink, and also are not immune from psychological disorders in general, they rarely drink in an uncontrolled way or become alcoholics. The low level of alcoholism amongst Jews in the U. S. A. would also appear to be the common experience in Britain. Bales believes that alcohol, especially wine, in a Jewish community stands for a whole complex of sacred things. It may be alluded to as the 'Word of God' and the 'Commandment of the Lord'. Drinking, like eating, has a sacrificial character, and is invested with an element of holiness. The dietary laws of Judaism are of more than religious significance in that they are symbolic of the separateness of the Jewish population. The Jewish child is thus instructed in 'correct' use of alcohol and food. To quote Bales: 'Drinking is thus sacred . . . and drunkeness a profanity'. The idea of drinking 'to become drunk' for personal reasons arouses strong culturally-induced counter-anxiety which renders uncontrolled drinking very unlikely. There are thus strong 'orientating' attitudes against the use of drink to relieve personal discomfort. There have been other sociological theories to account for the low rate of alcoholism in Jews. Thus Kant (quoted by Jellinek, 1941) put forward the 'in group verses the out group' hypothesis. This hypothesis proposed that Jews are afraid to drink because their civic position is weak and that because as an 'out group' they are subject to society's (the 'in group') hostility they are careful not to offend that society. Evidence supporting Bales's view comes from studies by Snyder (1962). Firstly, he found that as the religious affiliation of Jews moves from Orthodox to Conservative Reform to Secular, signs of drinking pathologies increase markedly, this increase not being attributable to social class or a difference in generation. Secondly, as young Jewish males move away from Jewish society to a Gentile one for long periods as on going to University or whilst on military service, their drinking behaviour approaches that of Gentiles. Snyder compares this pattern with the drinking pattern of Jews having regular business dealings with Gentiles. Here the Jewish drinking pattern is one of controlled drinking. He explains the difference is that in this situation as compared with that above emotional relationships between Jew and Gentile do not develop and the businessman returns at the end of the day to his strictly Jewish community. He is not cut off from his Jewish community nor is he developing strong emotional ties with non-Jews.

In Britain at the present time, as has already been stated, patients of Irish extraction appear to be overrepresented amongst alcoholics encountered in clinical practice whilst Jews appear underrepresented. Attention should also be focused on the drinking patterns of immigrant communities who have recently entered Britain. There would appear to be an underrepresentation of patients of West Indian, Indian and Pakistani origin in alcoholic clinics. Whether this represents a true prevalence of alcoholism in these ethnic groups or is due to their not coming forward for treatment can only be established by further field studies. It should be noted that in a study of prevalence of psychiatric disorders in South London amongst West Indian immigrants (Hemsi, 1967), there was a virtual absence of alcoholic patients. Extension of studies is urgently required, as are cross cultural studies of drinking behaviour between indigenous British citizens and citizens from these ethnic backgrounds. It would also be of considerable interest to see whether there is a shift in drinking patterns amongst young members of these ethnic groups away from those of their forebears to that of the young indigenous subjects as contact between the groups increases.

Jellinek (1960), in his monograph *The disease concept of alcoholism*, drew attention to the importance of social and economic factors in influencing drinking habits amongst different European nations and we have already mentioned 'spree drinking' in Finland, the 'fiesta drinking' of Latin countries and the steady drinking of the French (alcoholization). He emphasizes how in some countries alcoholism is regarded as having an 'economic origin' rather than 'psychiatric, psychopathological and physiopathological origins', as are emphasized in the Anglo-Saxon literature. Amongst economic factors are 'economic conditions of the individual, general economic depression of the country or pressure from a national economy in which the production and distribution of alcoholic beverages play such vital roles that they give an incentive to large individual consumption'. The first two factors relate to the importance of poverty leading to refuge in a tavern, and to the fact that generalized poverty with inadequate housing and associated misery will make people seek an escape in alcohol. The third factor refers to the political and economic pressures that are generated by a large section of the population being involved in the alcohol trade. Jellinek states, for example, that approximately one third of the French electorate are partly or entirely involved in the alcohol trade. Such interests encourage the large number of outlets for alcohol consumption; according to Jellinek there is approximately one outlet for every ninety-seven inhabitants.

Whilst such factors, particularly the size of the 'alcohol lobby' with its reluctance, to limit consumption by controls, may account for the high morbidity of the French population from alcohol, it should be noted that there are other wine-growing countries such as Italy, Spain and Argentina where alcohol problems appear much less serious despite there being a sizeable 'lobby'. Jellinek emphasizes that this difference may lie in differing social attitudes to the use of alcohol, and to such factors as tolerance of drunkenness in these differing populations. In France, Jellinek points out that alcohol as a beverage is held in high esteem. It is thought to be nourishing, high intakes are considered normal [in a survey by Bastide (1954), quoted by Jellinek, 2 litres of wine per day were acceptable to 48 per cent of males]. Further, drinking is spread throughout the day whereas in Italy (with a consumption approximately half that of France) drinking is confined to meals. In Italy, Jellinek emphasizes there is little social pressure for drinking whilst 'in France refusal to drink is met with hostility: further, drunkenness is regarded with contempt in Italy but much more tolerated in France.' These attitudes in France seem to resemble those of nineteenth century Ireland already described by Bales. It should be noted, however, that these observations of Jellinek are one to two decades old and there is evidence (de Lindt, 1973) that France alone amongst Western European countries has recently reduced her alcohol consumption *per capita*.

The awareness of the importance of social factors in society influencing alcoholism led Jellinek to postulate his 'vulnerability acceptance hypothesis'. Only the most psychologically vulnerable are likely to become addicted to alcohol in societies which 'orientate' away from the use of alcohol; in societies encouraging a large consumption, even moderately vulnerable individuals may become dependent. The lower incidence of alcoholism in women has been explained on this hypothesis in that orientating attitudes are more favourable to men than women in our culture.

Apart from the relationship between ethnic groups and drinking behaviour, recent attention as has already been outlined, has been focused (Edwards, Chandler and Hensman, 1972) on drinking behaviour in relation to sex and social class. It will be noted that in their drinking survey of an area in south London they examined six areas of different housing estates. Males tended to be heavier drinkers than females; features of alcohol dependence and stigmata of alcoholism such as drunken arrests were also commoner in males than females. Perhaps more interesting were the social class differences. As regards males, the upper social classes were lighter drinkers (I, II) than the lower social classes (III, IV, V); with women the reverse held true. Middle class males drank more often at home and in restaurants rather than in a bar of public house, which was favoured by working class members of the sample; however, middle class males were more likely to drink each day, whilst working class males were more likely to drink primarily at week-ends, when they would drink more heavily. Such heavy drinking in a public place renders them more likely to public displays of drunkenness, which may well lead to trouble with the law. Although for females there are broadly similar results in relation to social class, about half as many women as men (whatever the class) will give the public house as a preferred setting for consumption.

Clearly, studies such as these which require repetition in different parts of the country (as it is possible that within England different patterns may prevail in different regions in all social classes) emphasize the complexity of factors which shape drinking behaviour and as the authors state: 'It is impossible to describe a "typical" drinking pattern of "this suburb"—there are no typical drinking patterns.' Such facts have important implications for control of alcohol abuse, for, as is pointed out by the authors: 'The contrast between the drinking pattern of the I, II male and the IV, V female makes it starkly obvious that any taxation, education or other social manipulation which has as its imagined target the "typical British drinker" can do no more than discharge a blunderbuss.'

The social factors described above appear to explain the distribution rates of alcoholism in groups differentiated by socio-cultural parameters such as ethnic grouping and sex. They do not, of course, exclude the importance of personal factors but emphasize that such difficulties may well lead to problems with alcohol if socio-cultural factors present in an individual's development favour this.

REFERENCES

Bales, R. F. (1946). 'Cultural differences in rates of alcoholism.' *Q. Jl Stud. Alcohol* **6**, 480

De Lindt, J. (1973). 'The epidemiology of alcoholism: the elusive nature of the problem; estimating the prevalence of excessive alcoholism, and alcohol related mortality—current trends and the issue of prevention.' In *Alcoholism—a medical profile. Proceedings 1st International Medical Conference on Alcoholism, London.* London; B. Edsall

Edwards, G., Chandler, J. and Hensman, C. (1972). 'Drinking in a London suburb—I. Correllates of normal drinking. *Q. Jl Stud. Alcohol* supplement No. 6, p. 69

Field, P. G. (1962). 'A cross cultural study of drunkenness.' In *Society, culture and drinking patterns,* Ed. by D. J. Pittman and C. R. Snyder, New York; John Wiley

Hemsi, L. (1967). 'Psychiatric morbidity of West Indian immigrants.' *Social Psychiat. (Ger.)* **2**, 95

Horton, D. L. (1943). 'The function of alcohol in primitive societies: A cross cultural study.' *Q. Jl Stud. Alcohol* **4**, 199

Jellinek, E. M. (1941). 'Immanuel Kant on drinking.' *Q. Jl Stud. Alcohol* **1**, 777

Jellinek, E. M. (1960). *The disease concept of alcoholism.* New Haven, Connecticut; College and University Press, in association with Hillhouse Press, New Brunswick, NJ

Sangree, W. H. (1962). 'The social function of beer drinking in Bantu Tiriki.' In *Society, culture and drinking patterns.* Ed. by D. J. Pittman and C. R. Snyder, New York; John Wiley

Snyder, C. R. (1962). 'Culture and Jewish sobriety–the in group–out group factor.' In *Society, culture and drinking patterns.'* Ed. by D. J. Pittman and C. R. Snyder; New York; John Wiley

Ullman, A. D. (1952). 'The psychological mechanism of alcohol addiction.' *Q. Jl Stud. Alcohol* **13**, 602

W. H. O. (1952). *Tech. Rep. Ser. Wld Hlth Org.* No. 48, Expert Committee on Mental Health, Alcohol Sub-Committee. 2nd Report

4

AETIOLOGICAL FACTORS–
II. PHYSICAL FACTORS

The concept of a physical cause for alcoholism, whether this be genetically based or acquired, goes back many years. It has formed a major part of the viewpoint of members of Alcoholics Anonymous that alcoholism may be likened to diabetes mellitus and the alcoholic can be considered chemically different from his non-alcoholic peers. That such a viewpoint, with its removal of blame from the individual, has been of value to alcoholics is not contested; whether it is supported by evidence is another matter, and this will now be considered.

GENETIC FACTORS

Care has to be taken in discussing what one believes is inherited; in a genetic theory of alcoholism, is one primarily concerned with the inheritance of a specific (metabolic) syndrome or is one referring to the inheritance of basic personality types particularly vulnerable to alcohol dependence? This subject has been reviewed by Edwards (1970).

One theory (Cruz-Coke, 1965; Cruz-Coke and Varela, 1965) has attempted to link colour blindness with alcoholism. In 1965 Cruz-Coke described a highly-significant association between colour blindness and portal cirrhosis (alcohol-induced). He did not feel this could be explained by liver disease having interfered with the formation of eye pigments needed for colour vision. It was postulated that a connection existed in a sex-linked gene which might control a metabolic pathway in the pathogenesis of hepatic cirrhosis. Cruz-Coke and Varela (1965) then claimed that an association existed betweel alcoholics who *did not* have cirrhosis, and colour blindness. They suggested the genetic mechanism was an X-linked recessive trait and claimed that families of 20 alcoholics did show colour vision defects. Other workers comparing the incidence of colour vision defects in alcoholics with normal populations in England (Gorrell, 1967) and the U.S.A. (Thuline, 1964) have failed to confirm this finding.

Edwards (1970) has suggested reasons for the differences. They include questions of technical error, whether control groups were comparable or whether they skewed in terms of class and ethnic origin, and most important whether the alcoholic groups are comparable. He adds, 'The three research reports all seem strangely cavalier in their disregard of the need to define the condition under study'.

Apart from the 'colour vision hypothesis', another genetic hypothesis has been the 'blood group hypothesis'. This postulates a relationship between alcoholism and blood group. Again, results have been conflicting. Nordmo (1959) in the U.S.A., taking a large sample of alcoholics (of varying racial origins), found a highly significant (compared with a control group of blood donors) association between having a diagnosis of alcoholism, and Group A blood group status. However, in other countries (Finland—Achte, 1958; England—Madden, 1967, and Camps and Dodd, 1967) such a relationship has not been evident.

Classical techniques used to examine the relationship between psychiatric disorders and genetic factors are the method of comparing the incidence of that disorder in identical compared with non-identical twins, and the incidence of that disorder in different members of a family. Both these techniques have been applied in the case of alcoholism.

Kaij (1960) examined drinking behaviour of 174 twin pairs in Sweden (48 monozygotic and 126 dizygotic). Information was obtained from registers which denoted social consequences and from personal visits. Drinking behaviour was graded from minimal or no drinking to alcoholism. His results showed that 54.2 per cent of monozygotic twins were concordant for drinking habits whilst with dizygotic twins the figure was 31.5 per cent. These differences were significant. If only the cases of severe drinking habits were considered, then the concordance rate difference was even more evident. Kaij warns us, however, of drawing too rapid a conclusion, pointing out, 'The present study does not only concern chronic alcoholism but includes many persons with ordinary drinking habits. According to the conventional interpretation the findings of the study would imply that to a great extent, not only drinking habits but also the social manifestations of alcohol abuse are determined by genetic factors. . . . This does not necessarily mean that a number of genes or even a single gene substitution is related specifically to alcoholism. It may also be a question of unspecific factors of personality. To this question the present investigation can give no definite answer.'

Partanen, Kettil Brün and Mark-Kanen (1966) carried out an extensive study of twin pairs (902 in all) in Finland. They were examining drinking habits from interviews and records and also examined intelligence and personality variables. Data on drinking behaviour were subjected to factor analysis and three factors emerged. These were *density of alcohol* (this related to the frequency of use of alcohol, i.e. the part it plays in everyday life); *amount* (this related to the amount of alcohol consumed on a drinking occasion and to the length of a drinking episode and the degree of intoxication reached), and finally *lack of control* (this related to dependency and ability to control intake). They concluded that whether one drinks, how often and how much are to some extent determined by hereditary factors. On the other hand, the social consequences and arrests for drunkeness which are used to define alcoholism in Finnish society do not show any heriditary factors. In relation to the 'lack of control' factor they found that hereditary factors appeared important if young subjects were taken but not if older subjects were taken.

They finally draw our attention to the important point that hereditary factors vary in importance according to which aspect of alcohol intake is being considered, thus: 'If definitions are based solely on drinking behaviour and dependency on alcohol the presence of hereditary differences seems highly plausible. However if the criteria of alcoholism were, as currently in Finland and in many countries, based on social consequences of drinking there is no evidence for hereditary differences.'

ACQUIRED FACTORS

The idea of a primarily metabolic anomaly as the main cause of alcoholism would require the following. Firstly, the convincing demonstration of a metabolic anomaly which is significantly more often present. Secondly, this abnormality should be present in the early stages of alcoholism, particularly as metabolic abnormalities may arise in the later stages of alcohol dependence as a consequence of nutritional and metabolic change induced by prolonged drinking. Thirdly, the abnormality found in early stages of alcoholism should subsequently correlate with the development of alcoholism. It has to be admitted that such evidence has not been forthcoming.

One recent example of biochemical differences in a population in relation to alcohol has been the demonstration (Von Wartburg and

Pappenberg, 1970) that 20 per cent of a Swiss population and 4 per cent of a sample from London and Liverpool have an active enzyme variant of human liver alcohol dehydrogenase which *in vitro* increases the breakdown of alcohol. However, the frequency of occurrence of variant enzyme in an alcoholic population is not established.

REFERENCES

Achté, K. (1958). 'Correlations of ABO blood groups with alcoholism.' *Duodecim* 74, 20

Camps, F. E. and Dodd, B. E. (1967). 'Increase in the incidence of non-secretors of ABH blood groups substances amongst alcoholic patients.' *Br. med. J.* 1, 30

Cruz-Coke, R. (1965). 'Colour blindness and cirrhosis of the liver.' *Lancet* 1, 1131

Cruz-Coke, R. and Varela, A. (1965). Letter to the Editor, 'Colour blindness and alcohol addiction.' *Lancet* 2, 1348

Edwards, G. (1970). 'The status of alcoholism as a disease.' In *Modern trends in drug dependence and alcoholism*, Vol 1. Ed. by R. V. Phillipson. London; Butterworths

Gorrell, G. J. (1967). 'A study of defective colour vision with the Ishihara test plates. *Ann. hum. Genet.* 31, 39

Kaij, L. (1960). 'Alcoholism in twins.' In *Studies of the aetiology and sequels of abuse of alcohol.* Stockholm; Almquist & Wiksell

Madden, J. S. (1967). 'ABO blood groups and alcoholism.' Unpublished

Nordmo, S. M. (1959). 'Blood groups in schizophrenia, alcoholism and mental deficiency. *Am. J. Psychol.* 116, 460

Partanen, J. Kettil Brün and Mark-Kanen, T. (1966). 'Inheritance of drinking behaviour.' Finnish Foundation for Alcohol Studies, Publication No. 14

Thuline, H. C. (1967). 'Inheritance of alcoholism.' *Lancet* 1, 274

Von Wartburg, J. P. and Pappenberg, J. (1970). In Biochemical and enzymatic changes induced by chronic ethanol intake. *International Encyclopedia of Pharmacolocy and Therapeutics*, Section 20, Vol. 1. Oxford; Pergamon Press

5

AETIOLOGICAL FACTORS–
III. PSYCHOLOGICAL FACTORS

'Wine was the first anaesthetic–a nepenthic administered to cloud the imminence and mitigate the horrors of primitive surgery, and some of us are still inclined to take a "bracer" before asking for a raise, proposing marriage or undertaking some other presumably dangerous experience.'

Jules H. Masserman (1963)

Apart from the concept of a physical propensity in the alcoholic or potential alcoholic there is another model–the psychological one. This supports the view that psychological factors are primarily responsible for drinking behaviour, including alcoholism. Important reviews of this are by Conger (1956), Kingham (1958) and Orford (1971). The last of these is particularly useful and comprehensive in outlining the different types of psychological models that have been put forward. Orford emphasizes that alcoholism can be regarded as developing in *two* psychologically distinct steps. The first stage is the development of the habit of drinking which is often encouraged or not discouraged by society; the second is the maintenance of the habit despite contrary pressures by society. Orford suggests that three processes are involved in the learning of the habit. These are imitation, operant learning (instrumental learning) and classical conditioning.

Imitation refers to the copying of behaviour from a model. Social psychologists (e.g. Bandura and Walters, 1963) have emphasized how models are not picked at random but have certain characteristics. We choose models with whom we can strongly identify, such as parents, models who reward us, models whose status we envy and models whom we see rewarded (whether the reward is material or social). Parents satisfy many of these criteria. It is of interest that in line with previous work, in the study of *normal* drinking practices in London by Edwards,

31

Chandler and Hensman (1972), heavy-drinking males tended to have heavy-drinking fathers, and heavy-drinking females had heavy-drinking mothers. Parental drinking habits may influence drinking behaviour in two directions. Whilst the behaviour may be mimicked if parents are strongly identified with, reward their children, etc., if these factors are absent young people may not mimic parental behaviour. This does not apply only to drinking behaviour but to attitudes to drinking. It should be noticed that today advertisements, particularly on television, stress links between virility and drinking—drink is associated with virile, high-status models.

Operant learning (*instrumental learning*) refers to the well-known observation that a piece of behaviour which is rewarded is likely to be repeated, the converse also being true. The behaviour is 'instrumental' in bringing about the rewards. From the pharmacological viewpoint, in terms particularly of anxiety relief, alcohol may be rewarding. Drinking may also be rewarding in social terms, indeed society equates 'clubbiness' or '*bonhomie*' with drinking alcohol, certainly amongst males. In relation to anxiety relief and alcohol Orford (1971) emphasizes that two types of operant learning may operate. These are 'escape learning', in which anxiety already present is relieved by alcohol, and 'avoidance learning', in which anxiety not yet explained but anticipated is avoided through the use of alcohol. This latter type of learning according to Orford is particularly difficult to unlearn because it limits new ways of coping being discovered.

In animal experiments on operant learning, learning is stronger if reward (reinforcement) is intermittent rather than regular. The fact that the drinker with high anxiety is not always experiencing the same degree of anxiety and therefore does not receive the same degree of reward will strengthen behaviour. This 'intermittent reward' situation would appear to be more true to life.

Although these theories are attractive in relation to why some people drink and acquire the habit (i.e. drinking relieves unpleasant conditions), it has to be admitted that evidence in support is still limited. Studies pertinent to this have been carried out in animals and man.

Greenberg (1963) has induced stress reactions in rats by auditory stimuli. Such stimuli may result in manic behaviour, seizures and death ('audiogenic seizures'). Alcohol given to produce a blood concentration of 0.02–0.04% which is considerably below levels needed to induce intoxication in the rats or to produce any impairment of hearing, averted over 40 per cent of these seizures. It is of considerable interest to note that he points out, 'One does not find this response in all animals, even in all animals of one variety. In the rats that we used, about one out of every three randomly picked from the stock farm would be a responder.'

Masserman (1963) has studied extensively the effect of alcohol on neurotic reactions produced experimentally in animals such as cats. Such reactions are produced by placing the animal in a conflict situation, an example being training an animal to work a switch in return for a food reward and then placing the animal in an unpleasant situation by blowing air at it or giving it a mild electric shock. Such animals show both diffuse anxiety and phobias and startle reactions. These reactions can be markedly relieved by feeding the animal with alcohol.

It should be noticed that of all the animals which experienced an alleviation of neurotic symptoms during mild degrees of intoxication, approximately half began to prefer food or milk containing alcohol to plain food or milk. Masserman considers that they showed behaviour characteristic of 'alcohol addiction'. Conger, using rats in an approach– avoidance conflict situation, found that rats given intraperitoneal injections of water would not subject themselves to this situation whilst those given injections of alcohol did. A second experiment clarified that alcohol reduced the avoidance response rather than the approach response.

These experiments suggest alcohol in animals reduces stress (as induced by experimental stimuli) and avoidance behaviour in an approach–avoidance conflict, and that animals who 'learn' this effect of alcohol begin to prefer its ingestion compared with non-alcoholic beverages.

In relation to humans evidence of the importance of emotional relief from drinking is fragmentary and conflicting. Thus Knupfer (1963) in California found that heavy drinkers were those who drank to relieve unpleasant emotions. Neuroticism as measured on personality questionnaires such as the Eysenck Personality Inventory might be expected to be significantly correlated with drinking behaviour. However, in their survey of normal drinking in south London Edwards, Chandler and Hensman (1972) found that 'neither for males nor females is there a consistent relationship between QF* and mean N score'. Hore (1971), in a small number of alcoholic patients studied intensively in a prospective follow-up, was unable to find significant correlation between drinking behaviour and levels of anxiety. Further relapse was not associated with any significant changes in these levels in the 14 days preceding the onset of relapse. Kraft (1968) considered that for at least some alcoholics, their drinking behaviour was

*QF = Quantity/frequency index of drinking.

primarily a means of anxiety relief, and he attempted to relieve anxiety by other means, such as behavioural techniques. In the very small number of cases he reported on, this view appeared valid.

The arousal level of alcoholics in the absence of identifiable explicit environmental stimulation has been measured (Coopersmith and Woodrow, 1967), and compared with non-alcoholics using basal skin conductance as a measure or arousal. The numbers used were small, 8 alcoholics compared with 12 non-alcoholics. The results showed no significant difference between the two groups. The non-alcoholics when given alcohol had a reduction 30 minutes later of their general level of arousal. Greenburg (1963) has described measures of basal skin conductance in normal subjects before and after alcohol ingestion. After ingestion of 50 ml of alcohol there was a sharp fall in basal skin conductance. These experiments suggest that whilst alcohol reduces the general arousal level, the arousal level of the alcoholics in the absence of environmental stimulation is no greater than for non-alcoholics.

There are two further points in relation to operant learning that require mentioning. If drinking leads not to reward but punishment (non-reward), the habit is likely to be reduced. It is true that punishment may well follow but it is frequently delayed by many years. The use of non-reward (i. e. punishment) for drinking has been used for treatment (i. e. aversive treatment) and is considered later.

Classical conditioning refers to the formation of a new link between a stimulus and response. In the classic experiments of Pavlov, the sequence of the experiment was as follows:

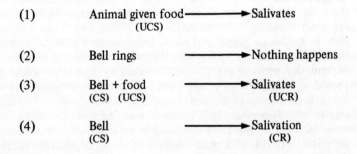

$$
\begin{array}{lll}
(1) & \text{Animal given food} \longrightarrow \text{Salivates} \\
 & \quad\quad\text{(UCS)} \\
(2) & \text{Bell rings} \longrightarrow \text{Nothing happens} \\
(3) & \text{Bell + food} \longrightarrow \text{Salivates} \\
 & \text{(CS)} \quad \text{(UCS)} \quad\quad\quad \text{(UCR)} \\
(4) & \text{Bell} \longrightarrow \text{Salivation} \\
 & \text{(CS)} \quad\quad\quad\quad\quad\quad \text{(CR)}
\end{array}
$$

UCS and UCR refer to unconditioned stimulus and unconditioned response respectively, whilst CS and CR refer to conditioning stimulus and conditioned response respectively. In effect the presentation of bell and food has led to a response which was not present before (i. e. line 4 compared with line 2). Such responses could be generalized, in that a response (of varying degree) was obtained from stimuli resembling but not identical with the original. In relating to drinking behaviour, the repeated presentation of visual and auditory stimuli (for example, the 'sights and sounds' of the bar or public house with alcohol, which itself produces a response such as anxiety relief or euphoria, may eventually lead to these stimuli themselves producing such effects. Clearly generalization may lead to a variety of stimuli working towards strengthening of the habit.

The second stage of the psychological theory is the maintence of the habit despite strong contrary pressures on the individual. Pressures may come from many sources but these usually include his spouse, relatives, friends, employers and agents of the state such as police officers. At this stage it is common to see denial and a tendency to project (Kessel and Walton, 1965) the blame for his condition on others. Orford suggests a factor in this denial is that such a patient is in a state of cognitive dissonance. This state, in which opposing attitudes and 'feelings' occur, is one in which there is a strong tendency to move away to reduce the dissonance. Denial and a refusal to accept the conflict will reduce dissonance and permit a more 'comfortable' state to be reached.

In the later stages drinking appears to be uncontrolled and it is common to talk of 'loss of control'. This has often been considered to be one of the criteria of the alcohol addict and this pattern has been considered to have a physical cause. Orford emphasizes that it can be approached from psychological theory, and that the conflict is one of the approach–avoidance type. In such a conflict there are two forces in opposition, a force tending towards the goal (i. e. drinking) and a force in the opposite direction. As the goal is approached the approach strength is greater than the avoidance as the approach situation is linked to stimuli which impinge *more* strongly. Up to the equilibrium point the avoidance strength outweighs the approach but beyond this point the approach tendency is the overall one. This is clearly an unstable situation and the person who approaches closely to the goal continues approaching until it is reached. This may be the reason behind advice given to alcoholics not to test themselves out by entering bars, standing next to others drinking, and so on. Orford considers this approach–avoidance behaviour is reminiscent to some degree of descriptions of 'loss of control', especially if this is not taken as meaning immediate loss. Orford also points out two further reasons why drinking may be maintained once the stage of dependence has been reached. Firstly, on 'operant learning principles' drinking behaviour may be maintained to stave off withdrawal symptoms. Secondly, as the forces influencing behaviour are related to the product of habit strength and drive level the development of physical dependence must increase drive level and therefore increase the tendency towards such behaviour (i. e. drinking behaviour).

In summary, theories based on learning suggest that drinking can be regarded as a habit which is acquired by three fundamental learning processes: imitation, operant (instrumental) and classical conditioning. Parental models are clearly important in the former and a recent survey of normal drinking practices would relate this to parents of the same sex. Models with a 'high virility content' are linked extensively with alcohol in advertisements.

Operant learning in this area relates to the rewarding effect of alcohol on unpleasant emotions, especially anxiety relief, in animals and man. Whilst it would seem that alcohol can reduce basal arousal level in man, and reduce 'anxiety' in animals, the importance of alcohol's effect on emotions in influencing drinking behaviour in humans still remains inconclusive. Classical conditioning responses, particularly in relation to generalization, may also play a role.

Although these learning principles will apply to everyone, different people 'experience' different models through development. They may also have differing levels of emotional reactivity or have had different attitudes towards alcohol induced in their childhood.

It should be noted that once the habit has started it is maintained with denial of the problem despite strong counter-pressure. Denial is afforded by cognitive dissonance. It is considered that once dependence of a physical type has been realized this will in itself increase drinking behaviour from the increased drive strength and also from the fear (non-reward) of withdrawal reactions. The ambivalent situation of the alcoholic can be seen as an approach–avoidance conflict, an unstable equilibrium, a type of equilibrium likely to lead to drinking reminiscent of the 'loss of control' type.

Apart from providing theories to promote understanding of the development of alcoholism, such theoretical formulations form the basis of techniques of treatment such as aversion techniques, which are considered later (Chapter 13).

REFERENCES

Bandura, A. and Walters, R. H. (1963). 'Social learning and personality develop-ment.' New York; Holt, Rinehart & Winston

Conger, J. J. (1956). 'Reinforcement theory and the dynamics of alcoholics.' *Q. Jl Stud. Alcohol* 17, 296

Coopersmith, S. and Woodrow, K. (1967). 'Basal conductive levels of normals and alcoholics.' *Q. Jl Stud. Alcohol* 28, 27

Edwards, G., Chandler, J. and Hensman, C. (1972). 'Drinking in a London suburb–I. correlates of normal drinking.' *Q. Jl. Stud. Alcohol* Supplement No. 6, p. 69

Greenberg, L. (1963). 'Alcohol and emotional behaviour.' In *Alcohol and civilization*. Ed. by S. Lucia. New York; McGraw-Hill Paperback

Hore, B. D. (1971). 'Factors in alcoholic relapse.' *Br. J. Addict.* **66, 89**

Kessel, N. and Walton, H. (1965). *Alcoholism*. London; Pelican Books

Kingham, R. J. (1958). 'Alcoholism and the reinforcement theory of learning.' *Q. Jl Stud. Alcohol* **19, 320**

Kraft, T. (1968). 'Experience in the treatment of alcoholism.' In *Progress in Behaviour Theory*. Ed. by H. J. Freeman, Bristol; John Wright

Knupfer, G. (1963). 'Factors related to amount of drinking in an urban community.' Report No. 6, California Drinking Practices Study, California, State Department of Public Health, 7151 Berkeley Way, Berkeley, California

Masserman, J. H. (1963). 'Alcoholism and neurotic behaviour.' In *Alcohol and civilization*. Ed. by S. Lucia. New York; McGraw-Hill Paperback

Orford, J. (1971). 'Psychological approaches to alcoholism.' Section—Community Medicine, *Update* (Aug. 1971), p. 1005

6

AETIOLOGICAL FACTORS-
IV. DEPENDENCE

Jellinek, in his classic monograph (1960), put forward the view that whilst early drinking behaviour is governed by psychological factors as already outlined, after a period of years physical dependency occurs and at this point certain phenomena become evident (Jellinek, 1960). These are increased tolerance to alcohol, the presence of a physical withdrawal syndrome (discussed in Chapter 10), craving for alcohol (already discussed in Chapter 2), and a drinking pattern characterized by loss of control and inability to abstain from alcohol. Loss of control refers to the subjective feeling of an inability to limit intake after the first few drinks. It was expressed well by a patient who said without prompting: 'Either I don't drink at all or if I do I cannot stop.' Such a pattern of drinking is likely to lead to intoxication and social difficulties, such as marital disharmony and trouble with the law. The 'loss of control' idea with the emphasis on immediate harm from 'one drink' has been a tenet of members of Alcoholics Anonymous and has been considered by some to be due to a biochemical disturbance. Merry (1966) gave 9 abstinent alcoholics alternate drinks containing disguised alcohol and water. There was no increase of craving as rated subjectively when the alcohol-containing beverages were taken. Merry considered that it was far more likely that environmental and psychological factors play a part 'more or less important than alcohol in the "loss of control" reaction'. Hershon (1973) and Orford (1971) as outlined in the previous chapter have emphasized that psychological factors more than physical are likely to be responsible for the loss of control phenomena.

Glatt (1972) has also re-examined this issue. Whilst agreeing with others that this is not primarily a physical disturbance he emphasizes how important total abstinence is for addicts. An attempt to control drinking in his experience usually leads eventually to loss of control, and some people die attempting it. In terms of psychological theories as already described, the loss of control phenomenon can be seen (Chapter 5) in terms of an approach–avoidance conflict. It should be emphasized that 'loss of control' is a subjective phenomenon and is by no means always clearly evident in patients complaining of physical withdrawal symptoms.

The inability to abstain refers to that pattern in which a high intake of alcohol is regularly taken. This may not lead to drunkeness but may well lead to physical complications such as cardiomyopathy, peripheral neuropathy and cirrhosis. In the author's experience this pattern is not uncommon in patients referred from medical clinics or wards.

Jellinek (1960) described the following different stages of alcohol dependence. Firstly, there is the *pre-clinical* phase where the stigmata of dependency are absent, and the drinking behaviour can be seen as learnt behaviour on the principle outlined above. As alcohol consumption increases we reach the next phase, the *pre-dependent* phase, with surreptitious drinking, feelings of guilt, a reluctance to discuss the drinking behaviour and the onset of amnesias for drinking periods (palimpsests; *see also* Chapter 10). The *dependent* phase proper then follows with drinking of either the 'loss of control' or 'inability to abstain' type. The former is commoner in Britain and North America, the latter more common on the Continent. Social disorganization occurs, including family difficulties, increasing alienation of friends, difficulties at work and with the law. The patient may become alcohol-centred, ensuring drink is always available. Each day frequently begins with a drink, one purpose of which is to prevent withdrawal symptoms such as morning tremor. The original psychological conflicts, social situation or need to test himself start the new bout of drinking.

The addictive phase leads to the *chronic* phase with frequent regular periods of intoxication, declining tolerance, social disorganization and in a minority of cases the appearance of alcoholic psychosis. The ultimate end is the 'Skid Row' alcoholic (Edwards *et al.*, 1966) which, however, occurs in only a minority of alcoholics.

Recent studies have suggested that alcohol dependence and dependence on opiates may have a common mechanism involving alterations in the metabolism of biogenic amines, particularly dopamine. Withdrawal syndromes may be based on this primary disturbance. These hypotheses have been reviewed in a recent *Lancet* editorial (*Lancet*, 1972). These hypotheses state that acetaldehyde derived from ethanol breakdown alters the metabolism of amines, including dopamine, producing aberrant metabolites having unique pharmacological activity. The breakdown, for example, of dopamine along this path involves a metabolic path that normally remains inoperative. It is stated that oxidation of an intermediate aldehyde produced in normal dopamine breakdown is inhibited by ethanol. Acetaldehyde (the prime metabolite of alcohol) is thought to block by competitive inhibition the normal conversion of amine-derived aldehyde to its corresponding acid. Elevation of these intermediate amine-derived aldehydes may then occur particularly in areas such as brain where there is low aldehyde oxidizing activity. These intermediate aldehydes may combine with parent amine, producing compounds resembling opiates such as morphine. Davis and Walsh (1970) have suggested that one such compound, tetrohydropapaveroline, which resembles morphine may be the compound *in vivo* and this compound might form the basis of ethanol addiction. The well-known clinical observations that alcohol addicts take opiates for relief of withdrawal syndromes and vice versa and that drugs used in relieving alcohol withdrawal syndromes, such as chloral hydrate or paraldehyde, also promote syntheses of products such as tetrohydropapaveroline.

Apart from dopamine it has also been claimed that other amines are similarly affected. Thus in the presence of ethanol, the intermediate aldehyde resulting from noradrenaline oxidation is shunted to an alternative pathway. At present there is little evidence from experiments *in vivo* to support these hypotheses but they may be the first tentative steps to an understanding of the manner in which alcohol induces dependence. As yet there is little understanding of how such compounds as tetrohydropapaveroline may be involved in the withdrawal reaction.

REFERENCES

Davis, V. E. and Walsh, M. J. (1970). 'Alcohol, amines and alkaloids.' *Science* **167,** 1005

Edwards, G., Hawker, A., Williamson, V. and Hensman, C. (1966). 'London's Skid Row.' *Lancet* **1,** 249

Glatt, M. M. (1972). 'The hazy borderline of the loss of control.' *Proceedings 30th International Congress of Alcoholism and Drug Dependence, Amsterdam, 1972.* Lausanne; International Council on Alcohol and Addictions

Hershon, H. I. (1973). 'Alcoholism, physical dependence and disease—Comment on "The Alcohologists, Addiction".' *Q. Jl Stud. Alcohol* **34,** 506

Jellinek, E. M. (1960). *The disease concept of alcoholism.* New Haven, Connecticut; College and University Press, in association with Hillhouse Press, New Brunswick, NJ

Lancet (1972). 'Alcohol addiction—a biochemical approach.' *Lancet* **1,** 24

Merry, J. (1966). 'The loss of control myth.' *Lancet* **1,** 1257

Orford, J. (1971). 'Psychological approaches to alcoholism.' Section Community Medicine, *Update* (Aug. 1971), p. 1005

7

PREVALENCE OF ALCOHOLISM

There are reasons other than academic interest as to why the number of alcoholics in any population should be known. Knowlege is necessary if services are to be logically planned, or even if alcoholism is to compete as a health priority (Edwards, 1973) its prevalence has to be satisfactorily documented. It is clear, however, that total numbers are only part of the information required as it is important to know which type of alcoholic exists in any community, and which kind of treatment facility these different groups are likely to use. Secondly, prevalence rates in different sections of society, for example different ethnic and socio-economic groups, may indicate sociological factors important in aetiology. Prevalence rates at different points in time may also indicate aetiological factors, and may assist in public health measures destined to reduce prevalence rates.

The application of epidemiological methods to alcoholism has been reviewed by several authors, including Straus (1952), Lipscomb (1959), Piedmont (1960), Mellor (1967), Knupfer (1967), Edwards (1973) and Wilkins (1974). Wilkins's study is of particular relevance to studies in general practice. Edwards (1973) also discusses the implication of epidemiological studies in terms of services. Studies of prevalence of alcoholism have certain inherent problems (Mellor, 1967). These include the lack of agreed definition of such terms as alcoholic, alcohol-dependent subject, problem drinker, etc. Indeed, as will be seen below a wide variety of definitions have been applied. Clark (1966) has shown how by altering definitions, prevalence rates can be made to vary considerably. Secondly, there is the fact that many people with drinking problems, and their relatives (perhaps to an even greater degree— Bailey, Haberman and Alksne, 1965; Wilkins, 1974) do not admit to such problems.

41

Prevalence studies have been of three main types. Firstly, the use of *indirect indices* (Lipscomb, 1959), such as alcoholic beverage consumption, social consequences linked with excessive drinking, arrests for drunkenness, traffic accidents, divorce rates, suicide rates, crime rates, mental hospital commitments, unemployment, disability rates, death rates and morbidity (i.e. the prevalence of illnesses known to be associated and number of people using services dealing with alcoholics. Also included in this category is the application of a formula (Jellinek formula) which attempts to obtain prevalence from the rate of alcoholic cirrhosis in a community. A further recent approach is that of De Lindt and Schmidt (1971), who emphasize how the size of the alcohol problem is related to overall consumption of alcohol in a country. Further, they define alcoholism as drinking more than 15 cl of absolute alcohol per day, this closely resembling the consumption of patients attending alcoholism clinics. The second type is the *enquiry from 'key personnel'* in any community of the number of alcoholics in that community that they know of. The final method is that of *surveys* of defined populations in relation to their drinking habits. With regard to the latter, it should be noted that in Britain with recent exceptions (Edwards, Chandler and Hensman, 1972; Ansvar Insurance Co., 1973), surveys have been of *abnormal* drinking, alcoholism, etc. rather than *normal* drinking.

INDIRECT ESTIMATES

As mentioned above, these include alcohol consumption figures, admissions to defined units such as mental hospitals, prevalence rates for illnesses associated with alcoholism, drunken offences and the use of an empirical formula (the Jellinek formula) to estimate prevalence rates. These matters have been well reviewed in the Office of Health Economics publication *Alcohol abuse* (O. H. E., 1970). *Figure 1* shows deaths from alcoholism, drunken offences and consumption of spirits and is reproduced from that publication. Whilst a relationship between consumption of alcohol and rates of alcoholism remains controversial and drunkenness offences rates may vary from time to time according to changes and enforcement of the law, the curves do indeed move in the same direction over a period of 80 years.

The Jellinek formula

This method (W. H. O., 1951) has been widely used throughout the world to estimate prevalence rates. It attempts to estimate the

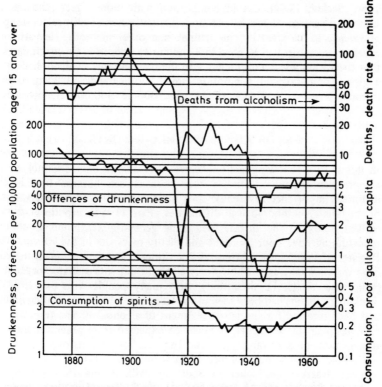

Figure 1. Deaths due to, or associated with, alcoholism, offences of drunkenness and consumption of spirits in England and Wales, 1875 to 1967. (From O. H. E., 1970 with permission of the Office of Health Economics)

prevalence of alcoholism using the frequency of cirrhosis in a community as an indirect estimate. The original Jellinek formula was $A = PD/K$, where A is the total number of alcoholics in that community for any given year, PD is the number of deaths that year from alcoholic cirrhosis and K is the percentage of alcoholics with complications who die from cirrhosis.

The formula was later modified to become $A = R \times PD/K$, where R is the ratio of all alcoholics to alcoholics with complications. It was necessary to modify the formula when it was realized that alcoholics existed who did not have such complications as cirrhosis.

It is likely that such a formula would still produce an underestimate as death certificates are likely to underestimate alcoholic cases of cirrhosis. The formula has been subject to critical reviews (Popham,

1956; Seeley, 1959), but in comparison with more direct methods surprising agreement has been found. Thus Popham (1970) calculated prevalence in 16 areas by the Jellinek and other methods. He found excellent agreement in 8, good in 3 and fair to poor in 5. He concluded that the formula was a useful guide to the total number of alcoholics in a given community at a point in time. For England and Wales the formula gives a prevalence of 11 per 1000 or 360,000 alcoholics.

USE OF 'KEY PERSONNEL' REPORTS

In this and the following section, 'Surveys', it is not intended to include all prevalence studies. Studies have been chosen because of their historical importance or because they indicate methodological variants or highlight methodological difficulties. Parr (1954) produced the earliest study in the British Isles using general practitioners as the reporting agency. Four hundred and eighty members of the Research Register of the College of General Practitioners were circulated with a brief questionnaire asking how many alcoholic patients each doctor had (using the W. H. O. definition), how many people with excessive drinking problems had been seen in the last year and how many patients had been referred for specialist treatment of alcoholism. The response rate was high (80 per cent), as might be expected from general practitioners motivated towards research. The rate for patients over 15 for the whole country was 1.1 per 1000 with a sex ratio 2.2:1 (male : female). Rates were higher in Scotland. Wilkins and Hore (1976) replicated Parr's study 18 years later in the Greater Manchester area. Defining problem drinkers and alcohol addicts, they circulated general practitioners who had referred at least one case of alcoholism to the Regional Addiction Unit. Although their response rate was disappointingly small (due perhaps to the remoteness of the investigations and the fact that the general practitioners were not motivated towards research), their rates resembled those of Parr. Further, when compared with a survey carried out in general practice in an area of Manchester (Wilkins, 1974) the ratios were one quarter to one sixth of the latter. Hensman *et al.* (1968) in a district of south London used general practitioners and clergymen as reporting agents. These clergy and doctors had all received education during the previous year. In relation to general practitioners, definitions used were those of the W. H. O. definition of alcoholism and a definition of the 'problem drinker'. The clergy were asked to define problem drinkers only. The rates were 5 male alcoholics per 1000 population aged over 20, and 1.7 female alcoholics per 1000 population aged over 20, according to the general practitioners. The clergy rate (problem drinkers) was 0.68 per 1000 population aged over 20. The 'educational programme' prior to the study probably accounted for the high response rate: 95 out of 98 general practitioners responded and all clergy who had agreed to participate did so.

These surveys mentioned so far perhaps suffer from 'overdependence on mailed questionnaires'. Grant and Boyd (1962), in a survey of the Down Hospital Area in Northern Ireland, interviewed each general practitioner personally using the W. H. O. definition. Even then, 3 out of 17 refused to co-operate. Their rate was 2.14 per 1000, resembling Parr's data and far lower than the W. H. O. estimate for England and Wales. They considered it unlikely that cases had been missed because of the 'intimate' nature of the country district being surveyed.

These British studies have shown an overreliance on general practitioners, a group who from direct surveys (e.g. Wilkins, 1974) appear quite likely not to detect alcoholism. One British study, that of Hawker, Edwards and Hensman (1967) using one group only, took a different group, namely employers. They circulated 279 firms in a London borough asking them about problem drinkers (which was defined) on their payroll at the time of the survey, those having left during the previous year and those having left during the previous five years. A high response rate was found (88 per cent). The authors were at pains to point out that the method was a way of arriving at 'visibility' rather than true prevalence. The results were 3.54 per 1000 males and 0.09 per 1000 females as problem drinkers in employment at that time; 2.43 per 1000 males and 0.03 per 1000 females as problem drinkers who had left in the previous year and 5.44 per 1000 males and 0.36 per 1000 females as problem drinkers who had left the firm in the previous five years. The rates would suggest that when compared with the W. H. O. estimate many cases of alcoholism in industry go undetected.

Studies using several groups of reporting agencies might be expected to show greater prevalence rates and provide a more accurate picture although cross duplication may occur; thus in a study of Monroe County, New York (Zax, Gardner and Hart, 1961) 32 per cent of the alcoholics identified had visited more than one agency. British studies using more than one agency include those of Hensman et al. (1968, already described), Prys-Williams and Glatt (1966), who used probation officers and health visitors in five English towns and extrapolated data to England and Wales, considering these estimates to resemble those obtained by the use of the Jellinek formula. Moss and Davies (1966) used 13 sources of information in the county of Cambridgeshire. The prevalence rate over a three year period (using definitions resembling in effect those of the W. H. O.) was 6.2 per 1000 males and 1.4 per 1000 females. Their criteria were regular or periodic heavy drinking and ill effects from drinking which had been observed during the study period. Their study also offered certain demographic data. Thus rates for both males and females were higher in urban than rural areas.

North American studies include those of Zax, Gardner and Hart (1961) and Gibbins (1954, 1968). Zax and co-workers *themselves* surveyed case records throughout 1961 of individual agencies dealing with alcoholics in Monroe County, including cases that had been placed on a psychiatric case register. Names and addresses were known, therefore cross duplication was avoided. Alcoholics were those who had been given a medical diagnosis of alcoholism, or had applied for service to an agency or clinic dealing exclusively with alcoholics or finally who had been arrested in 1961 on a charge of public intoxication. There perhaps is justification in doubting the validity of this last measure as an indicator of alcoholism. They also attempted to grade alcoholics in degrees of severity. In their results they describe how only 68 per cent of the alcoholics so identified had used a single agency. Apart from sex differences, they also compared rates in different ethnic groups, finding non-whites to have higher rates although these non-whites did not seem to use treatment agencies such as the Salvation Army or Alcoholics Information Centre as much as did whites.

Gibbins (1954) used interviews of nine sources of information in Ontario County, and cross checked names to avoid duplication. The prevalence rate during a six month period was 16 abnormal drinkers per 1000 of population aged 20 or over. Abnormal drinkers were composed of three groups (problem drinkers, alcohol addicts and chronic alcoholics), all of whom were clearly defined. It is worthy of note that only 7 per cent of the abnormal drinkers had ever undertaken treatment for their problem. Gibbins (quoted by Schmidt, 1968) acted as consultant to a second study in the same part of Ontario ten years later. The prevalence rate in 1961 (per 1000 adults) was 23 per cent representing an increase slightly more than 40 per cent. It should be noted that 22.8 per cent of the clients identified as alcoholics in the first survey were regarded as not being alcoholics in the second. It is worth emphasizing this in view of the widely held view that once a client has a 'drinking problem' this will invariably persist.

There are problems with the use of this type of 'key personnel' report. In effect these methods take into account alcoholics who have been in contact with social or treatment agencies; alcoholics who do not have that contact with these or any agency are of course missed. Secondly, the researcher is dependent on the ability of the 'key personnel' to identify alcoholics and in most groups this seems at the least doubtful. Thirdly, in large, ill-defined areas it may not be possible to motivate all groups, and if the records of agencies are to be searched the task may be immense. Fourthly, key personnel are likely to record not drinking behaviour but pathologies such as drunkenness offences (probation officers), cases of cirrhosis, delirium tremens, etc. (medical personnel). The greater the number of key personnel used the more accurate prevalence estimates are likely to be; however, there are still likely to be alcoholics who are missed, such as high income group patients who consult private physicians or attend nursing homes not sampled. Finally, as shown by studies such as that of Wilkins (1974), there seems to be definite underreporting by groups such as general practitioners.

SURVEYS

'The failure of investigators to ask the right questions is I believe a far more important source of error than the refusal of an occasional respondent to give an honest answer.'

Genevieve Knupfer (1969)

Community surveys

These form the second major group of prevalence studies, Strauss (1952) has described how even surveys with limited aims can delineate an alcoholism problem in a community and this can act as a spur to development of treatment services. Thus in 1949 a group of concerned citizens in Waterbury, Connecticut carried out a survey into the size of the problem in that area. After describing this, Strauss comments: 'The Waterbury survey at no time aimed at obtaining a complete count of alcoholics, or of the costs of alcoholism. It aimed merely to determine whether the problem was of sufficient scope to warrant the establishment of a clinic. When positive evidence was found this information was helpful in serving this facility.'

Knupfer (1967) has described difficulties inherent in the survey approach. Firstly, the survey team has to make its own definition of the type of drinking pattern it is looking for, whether this be problem drinking, addiction, etc. Such a measure should indicate not only the type of problem, but also the intensity and recency, that is, differentiate past and present drinking. In a survey of 1000 people representative of the actual population of San Francisco the problems the investigators found were separated into three groups, namely *social consequences* (job troubles, police troubles, troubles with friends, hospitalization and trouble with a spouse), *dependence* (own drinking seen as a problem, use of alcohol for coping and addictive symptoms) and *excessive intake* (prolonged drinks and frequent high index). The summary indices are shown in Table 1.

TABLE 1

Prevalence of Problem Drinking as a Percentage According to Indices, Varying by Intensity, Recovery and Type of Problem, in San Francisco. (After Knupfer, 1967)

	Serious—current	Serious—ever	Moderate or serious—ever
One or more signs of social consequences	2.1	4.0	10.0
One or more signs of dependence	7.0	7.4	19.9
One or both signs of excessive intake	3.1	14.1	20.8
One or more of the problems	15.9	18.9	33.1

Bailey, Haberman and Alksne (1965), in a survey of the Washington Heights Health District of New York County using house to house interviews, obtained data from a *single member of the family* about his or her own and other members' drinking habits. Subjects were asked, 'Have you or any member of the household had difficulty because of too much drinking?' Various areas of difficulty were specified. It is of interest that of the 99 who answered in the affirmative, 26 did not regard themselves as having current problems. This bears out the point made in Gibbins' follow-up study. Two further points of interest were the willingness of people to admit to their own problems more easily than to admit to problems in other members of the family; and that of the 99 clients already described, 50 had *never* sought help. This latter point resembles that made in the study by Gibbins already described in Ontario. The survey was able to examine prevalence rates in groups differentiated by sex, marital status, socio-economic background and ethnic groups. An overall prevalence rate of 19 per 1000 (for persons greater than 20 years of age) was found with a ratio of 3.6 men to 1 woman. Whilst the male : female ratio in whites was 6.2 : 1, in blacks it was 1.9 : 1 owing to the higher number of Negro women. It was felt that this increased rate amongst Negro women might be explained by a greater tolerance amongst Negroes of female drinkers and the more independent role, for example as heads of households, occupied by Negro women. Overall the most vulnerable sub-groups were widowers and divorced or separated people, and those with limited education. In relation to the latter, however, it was members of higher income groups that were overrepresented in a group who the researchers felt did have problems despite their denial.

A direct survey comparing results with those derived by the Jellinek formula was that of Manis and Hunt (1957). They picked an American town where it was felt that 'alcoholism isn't much of a problem'. Indeed this was a town that clearly felt proud of itself, as shown by the community's slogan 'Life is good in our town.' A random 2 per cent sample of households was made and questions related to difficulties from drinking. Despite the initial optimism at least 4.3 per cent of adults in the sample had experienced a serious drinking problem.

This point prevalence was compared with an estimate from the Jellinek formula made by computing cirrhosis death rates in that county over the last three years. The rate was 2.4 per cent. Once again this survey found very few of the people with problems had sought help.

Another early survey which also emphasized methodological problems as to what is abnormal drinking was that carried out by Marconi *et al.* (1955) in Chile. They used three criteria for problem drinking: frequency of drunkenness, habitual ingestion of alcoholic beverages before breakfast and frequency and duration of drinking sprees. The second criterion was eventually found to be useless as it could not be sharply differentiated from normal practice. Marconi and co-workers regarded 8.3 per cent of the males and 0.6 per cent of the females as alcoholics.

Surveys of specific populations

Two groups are described elsewhere. There are direct surveys in general practice, for example that of Wilkins (1974, Chapter 13), and surveys of criminal populations (Chapter 11). A third group is that of identifying alcoholics in general hospital populations. Such studies have examined series of patients admitted to medical wards with a variety of diagnoses and attempted to delineate the alcoholics amongst them. The criteria used have invariably been clinical. Thus Pearson (1962) used the presence of four out of six of the following criteria: blackouts, sneaking and gulping drinks, loss of control, morning eye-openers, loss of friends, family or jobs due to drinking, and hospitalization owing to drinking. Of 100 patients (aged 20 years or over) he found that 24 gave a positive history of alcoholism and in only 12 of these had the physician recorded the presence of the disorder.

Nolan (1965), using criteria similar to the W. H. O. definition, considered that 13 per cent of 900 consecutive admissions to the Grace New Haven Hospital, Connecticut, were alcoholics. Green in Melbourne (Green, 1965) examined 1000 consecutive patients using a screening device of six questions (relating to blackouts, 'eye-openers', loss of work time, feeling the need to drink, drinking at definite times, drinking on a spree). Following the screening, detailed questions were given to suspected cases. Alcoholism was defined as physical, mental or social incapacity produced by prolonged excessive drinking and 12.1 per cent of patients were considered to be alcoholics. Barcha, Stewart and Guze (1968) used a total of 16 signs and symptoms of alcoholism which fell into four main categories. Alcoholism was defined as a positive answer to a sign or symptom in three out of the four groups. These four groups were (a) blackouts, binges, tremors, delirium tremens or cirrhosis, and impotence; (b) loss of control of drinking, 'eye-openers', attempts made to control drinking, drinking non-beverage alcohol; (c) arrests, traffic difficulties, fighting and trouble at work; (d) loss of friends, the patient feeling he drinks too much, family protests, other protests and guilt feeling.

These studies on hospital populations have been reviewed by Ewing and Rouse (1970), who have made their own study of 130 randomly selected patients interviewed on medical and surgical wards. Each patient was asked questions which related to the definitions of alcoholism used by Pearson (1962) and Barcha, Stewart and Guze (1968). They found the highest rates of identified alcoholics were found (as perhaps was to be expected) using the criteria adopted by Barcha and co-workers, and that the criteria adopted by Pearson underestimated the rate as defined by the house officer looking after the cases. It was also apparent at least in this hospital that there had been an increase in the percentage of cases noted by the house staff in recent years. In their subsequent discussion they describe four symptoms they believe useful for a screening device. These are feeling the need to cut down drinking, annoyance towards people criticizing drinking, guilt about drinking, and requiring a morning drink to steady nerves or get rid of a hangover 'eye-opener'. The presence of all four answers in the affirmative is probably pathognomonic of alcoholism whilst three positive replies should create a high level of suspicion. Their studies suggest these criteria have some degree of validity and also because of their relatively innocuous quality are less likely to produce suspicion and resentment. These questions have the further advantage of being remembered under the mnemonic CAGE. It is disappointing to relate that such studies in Britain are conspicuous by their absence. A recent exception is that of E. P. Owens (personal communication, 1974). Preliminary findings from a prevalence study of alcoholism in men admitted to the medical wards of four general hospitals in Manchester suggest that *about 7 per cent* of male medical admissions are physically dependent on alcohol or have a serious drinking problem.

As with the use of 'key personnel' reports difficulties arise with survey techniques. Certain surveys concentrate on easily identifiable groups such as prison populations or hospital populations and can say little about the prevalence in an overall population. The perennial problem of definition remains. Clark (1966) has emphasized how as this varies prevalence rates vary. Difficulties can arise, as in the Santiago study (Marconi *et al.*, 1955), in differentiating abnormal drinking behaviour from normal. In community surveys difficulties may arise from sampling. One may be that alcoholics by virtue of their mobility may not be easy to count. Thus Hore, Wilkins and Alsfar (1976) in a validation study were able to obtain only a 25 per cent response rate when suspected problem drinkers and addicts were asked to return for a second interview. There may be denial of problems in different groups within the same survey (e.g. Bailey, Haberman and Alksne, 1966). Knupfer (1967) has emphasized how many studies do not record 'recency' and 'intensity'. Edwards (1973) emphasizes that surveys and also use of 'key personnel' reports are static. He states: 'There remains fundamental uncertainty as to whether the individual who is identified today as a problem drinker will in a year's time still be manifesting any disturbance.'

PRACTICAL VALUE OF PREVALENCE ESTIMATIONS

Edwards (1973) has reviewed the use in planning services of such data as described here. He warns that the limited services available for 'treatment' as evidenced by comparing prevalence estimates in a community with cases known to agencies should not automatically imply that 'our present treatment resources have simply to be multiplied up *n* times'. He doubts whether even if it were desirable, there will ever be enough trained personnel to deal with established cases and that what is needed is 'community research which will allow more accurate statement as to the nature of the case which ought to be referred to the treatment agency and the manner in which referrals and particularly self-referrals are to be made likely'.

REFERENCES

Ansvar Insurance Co. (1973). 'British drinking habits and some international comparisons.' Presented by G. Williams for the Ansver Insurance Co., *2nd International Conference on Alcoholism and Drug Dependence, Liverpool, 1973*

Bailey, M., Haberman, P. and Alksne, H. (1965). 'The epidemiology of alcoholism in an urban residential area.' *Q. Jl Stud. Alcohol* **26,** 19

Barcha, R., Stewart, M. A. and Guze, S. (1968). 'The prevalence of alcoholism among general hospital ward patients.' *Am. J. Psychol.* **125,** 681

Clark, W. (1966). 'Operational definition of drinking problems and associated prevalence rates.' *Q. Jl Stud. Alcohol* **27,** 648

De Lindt, J. and Schmidt, W. (1971). 'Consumption averages and alcoholism prevalence—a brief review of epidemiological investigation.' *Br. J. Addict.* **66,** 97

Edwards, G., Chandler, J. and Hensman, C. (1972). 'Drinking in a London suburb—I. Correllates of normal drinking. *Q. Jl Stud. Alcohol* Supplement No. 6, p. 69

Edwards, G. (1973). 'Epidemiology applied to alcoholism.' *Q. Jl Stud. Alcohol* **34,** 28

Ewing, J. A. and Rouse, B. A. (1970). 'Identifying the hidden alcoholic.' *29th International Congress on Alcoholism and Drug Dependence, Sydney, Australia, Feb. 1970.* Lausanne; International Council on Alcohol and Addictions

Gibbins, R. J. (1954). 'Alcoholism in Ontario—a survey of an Ontario county.' *Q. Jl Stud. Alcohol* **15,** 47

Grant, A. P. and Boyd, M. W. J. (1962). 'An assessment of the incidence of chronic alcoholism in Northern Ireland.' *Br. J. Addict.* **58,** 39

Green, J. R. (1965). 'The incidence of alcoholism in patients admitted to medical wards of a public hospital.' *Med. J. Aust.* **1,** 465

Hawker, A., Edwards, G. and Hensman, C. (1967). 'Problem drinkers on the payroll.' *Med. Offr* **118,** 313

Hensman, C., Edwards, G., Hawker, A. and Williamson, V. (1968). 'Identifying abnormal drinkers: prevalence estimates by general practitioners and clergymen.' *Med. Offr* **120,** 215

Hore, B. D., Wilkins, R. H. and Alsafar, J. (1976). 'An attempt at a criterion orientated validation of an alcoholism questionnaire in general practice.' *Br. J. Addict.* (in press)

Knupfer, G. (1967). 'Epidemiological studies and control programmes in alcoholism—V. The epidemiology of problem drinking.' *Am. J. publ. Hlth* **57,** 973

Lipscomb, W. R. (1959). 'The epidemiological methods in the study of alcoholism.' *Am. J. publ Hlth* **49,** 327

Manis, J. and Hunt, C. L. (1957). 'The community survey as a measure of the prevalence of alcoholism.' *Q. Jl Stud. Alcohol* **18,** 212

Marconi, J., Varela, A., Rosenblat, E., Solari, G., Marchesse, I., Alvarado, R. and Enriques, W. (1955). 'A survey on the prevalence of alcoholism among the adult population of a suburb in Santiago.' *Q. Jl Stud. Alcohol* **16**, 438

Mellor, C. S. (1967). 'The epidemiology of alcoholism.' *Hosp. Med.* **2**, 284

Moss, M. C. and Davies, E. B. (1967). 'A survey of alcoholism in an English county.' London; Geigy Scientific Publications

Nolan, J. P. (1965). 'Alcohol as a factor in the illness of university service patients.' *Am. J. med. Sci.* **249**, 135

O. H. E. (1970). 'Alcohol abuse.' Office of Health Economics, London, Publication No. 34

Parr, D. (1954). 'Alcoholism in general practice.' *Br. J. Addict.* **54**, 25

Pearson, W. S. (1962). 'The hidden alcoholics in the general hospital.' *N. Carol. med. J.* **23**, 6

Piedmont, G. B. (1960). 'A review of prevalence estimates for alcoholics.' *Int. J. soc. Psychiat.* **7**, 11

Popham, R. E. (1956). 'The Jellinek alcoholism estimation formula and its application to Canadian data.' *Q. Jl Stud. Alcohol* **17**, 559

Popham, R. E. (1970). 'Indirect methods of alcoholism prevalence estimation—a critical evaluation.' In *Alcohol and alcoholism*. Ed. by R. E. Popham, Toronto; University of Toronto Press

Prys-Williams, C. and Glatt, M. M. (1966). 'The incidence of long-standing alcoholism in England and Wales.' *Br. J. Addict.* **61**, 257

Schmidt, W. (1968). 'The prevalence of alcoholism and drug addiction in Canada.' *Addiction* **15**, 1

Seeley, J. (1959). 'Estimating the prevalence of alcoholism—a critical analysis of the Jellinek formula.' *Q. Jl Stud. Alcohol* **20**, 245

Straus, R. (1952). 'Community surveys: their aims and techniques with special reference to problems of alcoholism.' *Q. Jl Stud. Alcohol* **13**, 254

W. H. O. (1951). *Tech. Rep. Ser. Wld Hlth Org.* No. 42

Wilkins, R. H. (1974). *The hidden alcoholic in general practice.* London; Elek Science

Wilkins, R. H. and Hore, B. D. (1976). 'A general practitioner study of the estimated prevalence of alcoholism in the Greater Manchester area.' *Br. J. Addict.* (in press)

Zax, M., Gardner, E. A. and Hart, W. (1961). 'A survey of the prevalence of alcoholism in Monroe County, N. Y.' *Q. Jl Stud. Alcohol* **28**, 316

8

MEDICAL MORBIDITY

Although an association between illness and excessive drinking has long been recognized, the importance of alcohol as a significant factor contributing to the general morbidity of a hospital population remains insufficiently known. There are at least three probable reasons for this. Firstly, either the patient's unwillingness to confide to a doctor the truth of his drinking habits or perhaps genuine unawareness of his part of a drinking problem; secondly, the failure of the physician to elicit this information owing to his inability or unwillingness to ask appropriate questions; and thirdly, by the physician's incorrect stereotype of the alcoholic.

There have now been a few studies, however, which have attempted to assess the contribution alcoholism makes to the general morbidity of a hospital population. Let us consider two of the studies already mentioned in a previous chapter.

Nolan (1965) studied 900 consecutive admissions to the Grace New Haven Community Hospital in the U. S. A. Each admission was asked systematically by the house staff, questions relating to any functional interference by alcohol of their health, interpersonal relationships and economic status. It is clear these criteria relate to those of the W. H. O. definition of alcoholism. Nolan considered that 13 per cent of the patients were alcoholics, and that 10 per cent of admissions were due to diseases in which alcohol played a major aetiological part, and a further 0.4 per cent were due to diseases in which alcohol was probably an aetiological factor. When the alcoholic groups of patients were compared with the non-alcoholic they were found to be suffering significantly more frequently from the following diseases: acute bacterial pneumonia, pulmonary tuberculosis, epilepsy, acute gastritis, acute pancreatitis and cirrhosis of the liver. The alcoholic groups also ran the risk of increased morbidity by significantly delaying their admission and discharging themselves against medical advice.

Green (1965) examined 1000 consecutive patients admitted to the wards of St Vincent's Hospital in Melbourne. A screening device of six questions (blackouts, 'eye-openers', loss of work time, feeling the need to drink at definite times, drinking when alone, drinking on a spree) was initially used. Patients who answered affirmatively to more than one of these were subject to a detailed questionnaire. Alcoholism was then diagnosed as physical, mental or social incapacity produced by prolonged excessive drinking. It was considered that 12.1 per cent of the patients were alcoholics and 3.4 per cent of total admissions were diseases in which alcohol was a definite aetiological factor.

Studies such as those of Blane, Overton and Chafetz (1962) in the U. S. A. suggest that there are social factors there which enter into a physician's diagnosis of alcoholism. Blane and co-workers became aware that a large proportion of patients who could be considered alcoholics were not assigned to a treatment project for alcoholics. Examination of cases that were missed compared with non-missed showed that two sets of attitudes in the physician appeared to be responsible. The first was 'the physician's preference for a medical diagnosis rather than one which included social psychological factors' while the second was 'the physician's tendency to see alcoholism as a disorder that occurs primarily among socially isolated and impoverished chronic inebriates'. If the latter is true it means that the end state of alcoholism becomes the only form recognized. It is as if cancer were recognized only when metastases have become widespread.

Blane and co-workers looked carefully at two hypotheses. Cases of alcoholism in which the diagnosis had been missed would show fewer social characteristics of the 'Skid Row' type compared with cases not missed. Secondly, cases which had been missed were more likely to have been given a diagnosis of physical illness. The results showed that 'missed' cases were more likely to be married, to be employed, have a spouse, live at same address as their nearest relative, more likely to have medical insurance and were less likely to have come in under police escort. With regard to the second hypothesis, the missed cases would have a higher incidence than the assigned cases of patients given a medical diagnosis and would be more likely to have been missed. The important implications for management of alcoholism which are derived from this study are considered later. Clearly, however, such factors will discourage early cases of alcoholism from receiving treatment and particularly among physicians will create therapeutic pessimism. The importance of realizing that the alcoholic in the early stages of his illness is hidden and in social terms not very different from his non-alcoholic peers cannot be overemphasized. It was supported by studies of patients attending alcoholic clinics in the U. S. A. (Strauss and Bacon, 1951), patients attending alcoholic units in England and Wales (Hore and Smith, 1975) and information centres (Edwards *et al.*, 1967a). Strauss and Bacon (1951) examined 2023 male patients attending nine outpatient alcoholic clinics in the U. S. A. Over half of these patients were married and living with their wives when first seen in the clinics. The percentage who had never married was no greater than the normal expectancy. Three out of four men were living in an established household. Nine out of ten had lived in their present town of residence for at least ten years and nearly two thirds were gainfully employed. They suggest that 'from the findings of the present study it can be concluded that this segment of alcoholics, consisting of men who have maintained a high degree of family, community and occupational integration although hitherto not identified, is perhaps the most significant element in the entire alcoholic population.'

Edwards *et al.* (1967a) devised a questionnaire administered by the staff of information centres to 300 clients (164 males, 36 females) attending such centres in three cities in England. Of the clients, 48 per cent were married and living with spouses, 32 per cent had never been on a drinking charge, 50 per cent were in employment, and 49 per cent had been with their employer for more than two years. They emphasize how these clients differ from those of London's 'Skid Row' and that they are very largely citizens with a normal background and social integration. A similar pattern was seen in patients attending Alcoholism Treatment Units in England and Wales (Hore and Smith, 1975).

The remainder of this chapter deals with the various diseases associated with excessive alchol intake.

GASTRITIS

There would seem little doubt that alcohol can induce acute gastritis. Wynn Williams (1956) has produced these changes experimentally in animals. He studied the effect of graded concentrations and volumes of ethyl alcohol on the stomach wall in guinea-pigs. As regards concentrations of alcohol, changes were pronounced when 40% alcohol was given; these changes included multiple haemorrhages, erosion and ulceration of the mucosa, together with loss of weight, and fatty change in the liver. The gastric lesions were primarily concentrated in the upper two thirds of the stomach. With high concentrations of alcohol (60%) hyperaemic changes occurred after half an hour, and at an hour necrosis of the mucosa occurred. Fasting of animals in general increased the severity of mucosal lesions produced by alcohol, as did increasing the volume of alcohol. He concluded that 'although the amounts of alcohol administered to the guinea-pigs were relatively very large compared with those consumed by the majority of human subjects, it may be reasonable to assume that the consumption of large quantities of the more concentrated alcoholic drinks may lead to haemorrhage, erosion and ulcers in humans especially if the drinks are taken on an empty stomach.'

Palmer (1954), in a general review of gastritis, draws attention to the early direct observation by Beaumont that St Martin's* alcoholic sprees led to reversible mucosal inflammation and excessive secretion. Palmer examined 34 patients with severe alcoholism by means of gastroscopy within six hours of their last drink. Thirty showed changes caused by acute exogenous gastritis. In 23 of these patients examined after 7–21 days of abstinence there was, however, a return of the mucosa to normal.

Wynn Williams (1956) examined gastric mucosa taken from 25 alcoholics. Normal mucosa was present in 9 patients, mild to moderate inflammatory changes in 7 and chronic changes of atrophic gastritis in 6. Six patients showed peptic ulceration.

Whilst it would appear from animal and human studies such as those described that alcohol can induce acute gastritis, opinion as to the importance of alcohol in causing chronic atrophic gastritis, that is, glandular atrophy and round cell infiltration, remains controversial. Studies of alcoholics include some finding an increased incidence of chronic gastritis greater than expected by chance and some finding the opposite. Wyn Williams (1956) considered, 'It is possible, therefore, that in a proportion of stomachs with chronic atrophic gastritis the latter may be attributable, at least in part, to chronic alcohol excess.' Palmer (1954) was, however, more definite in stating that there is no substantial clinical or pathological evidence to permit one to lay the blame for chronic gastritis on alcoholism. Further experimental attempts to produce chronic alcoholic gastritis have failed.

Wood and Taft (1958) consider that various studies may have produced different results because of different means of selecting

---

*St. Martin was an experimental subject who had a fistula which enabled direct examination of the stomach lining to be made.

patients. They consider that serial gastric biopsies in patients who continue drinking often progress from superficial to severe atrophic gastritis. Different series of patients may thus, according to the length of drinking history, show different degrees of severity of gastritis.

PEPTIC ULCERS

The relationship between alcohol and these two common disorders (viz. gastric and duodenal ulcers) has been examined in two ways. Firstly, the frequency of peptic ulcer in alcoholic populations has been compared with control populations. Although the incidence of peptic ulcer has been reported to be relatively high in several studies, occurring in 8 out of 47 'Skid Row' alcoholics (Edwards *et al.* 1966) and in 19 per cent of 246 males and 21 per cent of 58 females attending Alcoholics Anonymous (Edwards *et al.*, 1967b), although since this was not related to control data its significance remains uncertain. Further criteria for the diagnosis of peptic ulcer may require more than an anecdotal history from the patient. Engeset, Lyrgren and Idsoe (1963) examined a group of 251 alcoholics and 329 non-alcoholics, matched for sex and age distribution in the same town in Norway. The patients were examined clinically and radiologically and ulcer diagnosed only if shown definitely on X-ray or at operation. More ulcers (gastric plus duodenal) were found in the alcoholic population than in the control group, the difference being significant at the 5% level. For duodenal ulcer alone, there was not a significant difference. Using 'softer' data, namely patients' histories for evidence of peptic ulcer, Hagnell and Wretmark (1957) in 130 alcoholics found that in Sweden the frequency of peptic ulcer was greater than the expected frequency in a Swedish population. Similarly, Pell and d'Alonzo (1968), examining prevalence of chronic disease amongst 922 employees of a large American company who were suspected problem drinkers (and using patients' histories), found, compared with a control group (matched for age, sex, occupation and geographical location), that the prevalence of gastric ulcer was higher in the problem drinking group at a level of 1% significance. With duodenal ulcer the significance was at 5%.

A contrary view to the studies above was that of Bingham (1960) in Canada. He examined 430 chronic alcoholics who, apart from drinking alcohol, behaved in a way likely to increase ulcer formation and/or encourage the persistence of an established ulcer, that is, they drank coffee, smoked and led irregular lives. The incidence of peptic ulcer (5.3%) was not higher than that expected in the general population (5–10%). He concluded that peptic ulcer was no more common than amongst the general population.

The second method of examination has been to compare the frequency of alcoholics amongst a peptic ulcer population with a control group. Thus Retterstol and Sund (1962) in Norway found that the incidence of alcohol abuse in peptic ulcer patients seen at a psychiatric clinic was three times that of a control group of psychiatric patients who did not have peptic ulcer.

PANCREATITIS

In the U. S. A., prolonged alcohol ingestion is regarded as one of the two major causes of pancreatitis (Bockus *et al.*, 1955; Howard and Ehrlich, 1960). Bockus *et al.* (1955), in a review of 94 admissions in 78 patients, found that for 41 admissions (31 patients) significant prior alcohol intake had occurred. They considered that acute pancreatitis of alcoholic origin could be differentiated from 'biliary pancreatitis' (the other major cause) in being more severe with more prolonged elevation of the serum amylase level, having a greater incidence of complications including pancreatic ileus and pancreatic calcification, and more likely to be followed by recurrent attacks. Chronic pancreatic insufficiency is also more likely to follow. Alcohol as a precipitating factor was implicated in 18 per cent of the 307 cases described by Paxton and Payne (1948). In these cases the patients were either admitted intoxicated or were recuperating from a drinking bout. Cogbill and Taek-Song (1970), in another American study of 147 cases of acute pancreatitis, considered 53 per cent of cases were suffering from alcoholism although this was not defined. Using autopsy material Weiner and Tennant (1938), in one of the earlier studies, concluded that in 38 cases of death from acute haemorrhagic pancreatitis, in 25 of the patients alcohol had been a precipitating factor. Although estimates vary, these studies taken from the U. S. A. implicate alcohol as an important precipitating factor and alcoholics as a group especially prone to this disorder. The one major study in Britain reached the opposite conclusion. Pollock (1959) in Leeds looked at 1000 patients with acute pancreatitis and was unable to find any single case of alcoholism. It should be noted that the criteria for alcoholism were not described. It is difficult to explain this difference in terms of different proportions of alcoholics in England and American populations. The work of an alcoholic out-patient clinic in a town near Leeds (Smith-Moorhouse and Lynn, 1969) would suggest that alcoholics exist there as well as anywhere else in Britain.

To look at this association the other way round, there is evidence of an increased rate of pancreatic dysfunction in alcoholics, at least in the

U. S. A. Thus Domzalski and Wedge (1948) found that 24 per cent of 50 alcoholics had an elevated serum amylase level compared with 2 per cent of a control group of equal numbers, whilst Weiner and Tennant (1938) found that of 51 patients dying during acute alcoholic episodes 22 (55 per cent) showed pancreatic lesions. In a group of 41 patients dying from chronic alcoholism, 14 (41 per cent) showed pancreatic lesions.

HEPATIC DISEASE

Recent reviews of this subject include those of Melmed (1967), a *Lancet* editorial (1968) and Clark (1973). Both acute and chronic syndromes exist although the latter—fatty liver and cirrhosis (Clark, 1973)—are better known. Acute alcoholic hepatitis (Melmed, 1967) may follow intensified drinking in the chronic alcoholic and may carry a grave prognosis. It is characterized by anorexia, nausea, vomiting, upper abdominal pain with the signs of tender hepatosplenomegaly and persistent pyrexia. Differentiation from other causes of hepatitis is aided by a positive history of alcoholism, persistent pyrexia, severe pain, a grossly enlarged liver and on laboratory examination a polymorpholeucocytosis with less evidence of liver damage on liver function tests than is usually evident with infectious or serum hepatitis. Chronic liver disease takes the form of alcoholic fatty liver (ranging from microscopic with no impairment of function to marked accumulation with derangement of function).

The mechanism by which alcohol injures the liver has been disputed. A common early view was that the injury was the result of nutritional deficiencies, such deficiencies commonly occurring in the alcoholic with his well-known lack of appetite and use of alcohol as a calorie source. Recent studies have challenged this viewpoint. Rubin and Lieber (1968) gave five alcoholic volunteers alcohol, together with an adequate high-protein, low-fat diet. Similar studies were carried out on non-alcoholic volunteers. Despite the adequate diet, fatty change and ultrastructural changes observed on electron microscopy occurred. The levels of blood alcohol were low, averaging around 50 mg%. Direct damage from alcohol cannot, however, be the only factor, for Phillips, Gabuzba and Davidson (1952) showed that in three alcoholics abstinence and adequate protein failed to produce an improvement in hepatic function. Leevy and Ten-Hove (quoted in a *Lancet* editorial, 1968) found that even if alcohol was continued, improvement in hepatic function occurred if an adequate protein diet was given.

The contribution that the degree of drinking (in terms of quantity and frequency) makes to improved liver function was estimated in an important study by Lelbach (1966). A linear relationship was found between the severity of changes in hepatic function, and the duration and dose of alcohol. Powell and Klatskin (1968) have demonstrated that abstinence is advantageous as regards improving liver function in the cirrhotic. Of 93 patients with a histologically proven diagnosis of cirrhosis 64 per cent survived for five years. This compared with a five year survival rate of 40 per cent in 185 patients who continued to drink despite advice to the contrary.

Besides the association between alcohol and acute hepatitis, and alcohol and cirrhosis, two other conditions should be considered. Zieve (1958) has described a syndrome in males in which heavy ingestion of alcohol was associated with the development of jaundice, hyperlipaemia and haemolytic anaemia. The hyperlipaemia may occur independently of the other features. Secondly, there is an association between alcohol and haemochromatosis (Melmed, 1967). McDonald (1964, 1965) has emphasized the importance of alcohol as a factor in this disorder. In countries such as France where alcohol intake is high, as is cirrhosis, the incidence of haemochromatosis is relatively very high, and amongst patients with haemochromatosis alcoholism has been reported in almost 30 per cent (Melmed, 1967). McDonald (1965) in animal experiments has demonstrated that folic acid deficiency may be an important factor in producing iron deposition; alcoholics themselves may of course be folic acid-deficient.

PULMONARY TUBERCULOSIS

A link between alcohol and tuberculosis has been supported by studies from Britain and Canada. Lewis and Chamberlain (1963) examined 100 consecutive cases of pulmonary tuberculosis and compared this with two control groups matched for age and social class. They found that a significantly greater number of patients (at the 1% level) in the tuberculosis group compared with the control groups were regular drinkers. A 'regular drinker' was one who drank two pints of beer or more daily. Drinking behaviour was that described by patients, and relatives were not interviewed. Pincock (1964) examined 306 patients admitted to the in-patient unit of a tuberculosis clinic in Winnipeg; patients and relatives were questioned regarding the drinking habits of these patients. Using a definition of alcoholism akin to that of the W. H. O. (see Chapter 1) and also the term 'problem drinker', they found a prevalence rate in these groups combined equal to five times that of the non-tuberculous population. They also claim that an early relapse and readmission to a sanatorium can be anticipated in patients who return to their former pattern of drinking. Olin and Grzybowski (1966) examined a group of chronic drunken offenders. In 202 out of the sample of 227 chest X-rays were carried out and evidence of tuberculosis sought. A similar investigation was carried out on a non-alcoholic matched group. The films were marked independently. A second study compared the results of tuberculin testing in an alcoholic group and matched controls. Both studies showed a significant greater increase in tuberculosis in the alcoholic group. These authors emphasize the association between tuberculosis and alcoholics of the 'Skid Row' population and Pincock (1964) considered that the factor linking alcoholism and tuberculosis was most likely an indirect one, namely that of poor socio-economic conditions. Alcoholics receiving in-patient treatment for tuberculosis bear out a general statement made earlier by Green (1965), namely that they may be uncooperative and unreliable and discharge themselves before treatment is completed. Indeed Olin and Grzybowski suggest treatment for such patients in special settings.

CARDIAC DISEASE AND EXCESSIVE ALCOHOL INTAKE

The subject has recently been well reviewed by Sanders (1970). Alcohol is considered to be a cause of primary congestive cardiomyopathy. In such cases (Sanders, 1970), it is important to exclude cases of beriberi heart disease by taking an adequate dietary history. Clinical presentation is usually of congestive cardiac failure not attributable to valvular or arterial disease. It has been claimed that there are ECG changes, particulary T wave changes (Evans, 1964), which are pathognomic, but this is not agreed by all (Sanders, 1970), although it is agreed that ECG changes are extremely common. Electron microscopic studies have shown marked structural changes in the myocardium of patients dying from alcoholic heart disease, but it would appear that similar changes (*British Medical Journal* editorial, 1972) can occur in primary myocardial disease from which alcohol can be excluded as a cause. With regard to the mechanism of myocardial damage and alcohol, earlier studies attributed this to co-existent vitamin deficiency. Most patients in developed countries who present with alcoholic cardiomyopathy, however, would appear to be well nourished and not vitamin-deficient (*British Medical Journal* editorial, 1972).

A recent study by Burch *et al.* (1971) has shown that in mice alcohol can produce focal myocardial changes, the changes being similar to those described for human hearts and that they occur irrespective of the strength or type of alcohol used. Apart from the chronic cardiomyopathy an acute syndrome has been described in several centres. In one of these, Quebec, the cause was considered to be cobalt added to beer (Morin, 1966).

ALCOHOL AND BLOOD DISORDERS

This subject has been the topic of a *Lancet* editorial (1969). It would appear that alcohol can affect the blood in at least four way. Firstly, there is the nutritional effect of a dietary lack of folic acid common in the alcoholic, and producing megaloblastic erythropoiesis. Secondly, alcohol may suppress erythropoiesis (Sullivan and Herbert, 1964), in the presence of folate. Thirdly, alcohol may interfere with the transport of iron (Sullivan and Herbert, 1964). Finally, alcohol itself can produce changes in the blood-forming cells. These include vacuolation of normoblasts, and the appearance of ring sideroblasts (McCurdy, Pierce and Rath, 1962; Hines, 1969).

ALCOHOL AND HYPOGLYCAEMIA

This syndrome, although described thirty years ago, is poorly documented. It has recently been reviewed (*Journal of Alcoholism* editorial, 1972) and by Bogdanski and Lindenaur (1966). The latter authors describe three cases and review others in the literature. The usual time for hypoglycaemia to occur is 12–72 hours after ingestion and it is usually associated with fasting. The blood alcohol levels may be low. In their series it averated 14 mg% whilst in the literature it averaged 30 mg%. The main clinical features were coma, spasm of extremities and bizarre neurological manifestations. These were reversible on giving a single injection of 20–70 ml of 50% dextrose solution. They consider that 50% glucose (after a blood sample is taken) should be given to all patients with unexplained coma. They add 'this method of treatment may well be life saving and will certainly not be detrimental when given for coma from alcohol or any other cause.'

Pawar (1972) reported on two elderly male patients (aged 67 and 82 years) who presented in coma with hypoglycaemia and hypothermia produced by drinking large quantities of alcohol (four pints of beer and half a bottle of whisky, and one and a half bottles of whisky respectively). The younger patient also appeared to have a history of dietary deficiency. Consciousness rapidly returned on administering intravenous dextrose but in one patient hypoglycaemia persisted for 24 hours.

Lündquist (quoted in the *Journal of Alcoholism* editorial, 1972) considers that such hypoglycaemia results in patients who have decreased glycogen stores and is the result of alcohol causing a further fall in glucose production. It would appear that in drunken comatose patients, apart from excluding such factors as head injury, attention should be paid to the blood glucose level especially as the condition is eminently reversible by simple measures, as Bogdanski and Lindenaur have stated.

NEUROLOGICAL SYNDROMES

An outstanding review is that of Victor (1962), which includes extracts of original descriptions of the well-known neuropsychiatric syndromes. Other reviews are by Lees (1967) and Hore (1973). The major psychiatric syndromes will be described in Chapter 10.

The neurological syndromes can be simply divided as follows (Victor, 1962).

Syndromes due to a direct effect of alcohol

Perhaps the commonest of these is intoxication due to ethyl alcohol. The symptoms are well known and primarily involve disturbances in gait, balance and speech and may be accompanied by emotional changes. The effects of alcohol on physiological functions, for example neuromuscular, ocular, etc. have been reviewed (Havard, 1963). Although the majority of cases recover, fatalities from depression of basal centres may occur. Acute intoxication due to methyl alcohol, although less well known and largely confined to deteriorated alcoholics drinking methylated spirits, may lead to serious complications. The well-known picture of intoxication by ethyl alcohol is accompanied by abdominal and visual symptoms, the latter being a precursor of bilateral retrobulbar neuritis which may lead to blindness.

Coma in the alcoholic may arise from causes apart from hypoglycaemia and the direct depressant effect of alcohol on cerebral function. These include head injury resulting in lesions such as subdural haematoma, and post-epileptic coma. The importance of alcohol-induced hypoglycaemia in that it is easily reversible has already been described.

Syndromes due to the withdrawal effect of alcohol in the alcohol-dependent subject

Controversy over the ability of alcohol to produce physical dependence has been resolved by the studies of Isbell *et al.* (1955) and Mendellson

(1964). Isbell and co-workers found in a group of prison volunteers given large quantities of alcohol for periods ranging from 7–57 days that abrupt cessation of intake in those subjects who had taken drink for at least 48 days caused severe withdrawal syndromes characterized by epileptic fits and the features of delirium tremens. Mendellson (1964), using 10 subjects who drank whisky for 24 days, confirmed these findings. The majority of subjects showed tremors and hallucinations. Victor and Hope (1958) and Victor (1971) have described in detail the gradation of the alcohol withdrawal syndrome. Withdrawal of alcohol in a physically-dependent subject may lead to one or more of the following features. These include the morning shakes, general irritability, nausea and vomiting which may be isolated, hallucinations, fits ('rum fits') and delirium. 'Morning shakes' refers to the tremulousness of the limbs, especially upper limbs, on arising in the morning after a drinking episode the night before. The tremor is often coarse and affects pronator and supinator movements. It differs from the tremor of hepatic failure in that the latter appears to involve flexor and extensor movements. The tremor may be so severe that a cup cannot be held without spilling the contents. The tremor will often be relieved by ingesting alcohol, as the patient rapidly learns. The 'morning shakes' is an important symptom in that it indicates that a stage of physical dependence has been reached. Epileptic fits may occur as isolated phenomena or as part of delirium tremens. Reports linking epilepsy and alcoholism go back many years. Glatt in 1955 reported that 22.7 per cent of 110 male alcoholic patients and 10 per cent of 50 female alcoholic patients admitted to a history of convulsions. Danesin (1970) examined 321 chronic alcoholics admitted to a regional hospital. Forty-one (15 per cent) developed epileptic fits after more than two years of addiction although they gave no history of neurological disorder or epilepsy prior to drinking. The average age of the onset of seizures was 35 whilst drinking was mainly wine in the form of 2–3 litres per day. Danesin considered that fits could occur in bouts of heavy drinking as well as in withdrawal periods. Lees (1967) has reviewed the causes of epilepsy in association with alcoholic intake. These include those arising as part of acute intoxication, as an isolated withdrawal phenomenon or accompanying other features of the withdrawal syndrome: hypoglycaemia, arising from alcohol-induced brain damage (recent reports suggest brain damage as evidenced by cerebral atrophy is much commoner than was previously thought—see Chapter 10) and as a precipitant in a known epileptic. More than one factor may induce a fit. The author recently saw a middle-aged alcohol-dependent subject with no previous history of epilepsy who during a voluntary withdrawal phase had his first grand mal attack whilst he watched flickering illuminations at a seaside town.

The syndrome of delirium tremens is considered in Chapter 10.

Syndromes believed to be due to associated nutritional deficiencies

These include Wernicke's encephalopathy, Korsakoff's psychosis, alcohol-induced brain damage and peripheral neuropathy. All but the last of these are considered in Chapter 10. Peripheral neuropathy in relation to alcohol has been reviewed by Victor (1962), Lees (1967) and Mawdsley and Mayer (1965). Victor (1962) points out that although an association had been known before the beginning of this century, it was Shattuck in 1928 (cited by Victor, 1962) who first emphasized the nutritional aetiology of beriberi. The aetiology of alcoholic peripheral neuropathy would not appear to be fully settled. Victor, after describing how such a neuropathy can occur in animals (rat, dog and pigeon) made deficient in B group vitamins such as thiamine, pyridoxine and pantothenic acid, considered 'there is a small but convincing body of data which show that the clinical signs of neuropathy can be produced by a deficiency of thiamine, pyridoxine or pantothenic acid.' In their review, Mawdsley and Mayer (1965) describe their studies on nerve conduction velocity in alcoholics and normal controls. The alcoholics comprised those *without* signs of peripheral neuropathy as well as those with peripheral neuropathy. Considering those without signs of neuropathy first, there was a significant slowing compared with normals in both young (under 50 years) and elderly patients (greater than 50 years). As expected amongst patients with neuropathy there was also a reduction in velocity compared with normals. In discussing the aetiology of alcoholic peripheral neuropathy Mawdsley and Mayer generally agree with Victor; whilst stressing the importance of thiamine deficiency they consider that pyridoxine and pantothenic acid deficiency may also be factors.

Pathological changes include segmental demyelination without the destruction of axis cylinders. According to Lees (1967) the process begins peripherally. In severe cases Victor (1962) described destruction of anterior and posterior nerve roots. Alcoholic peripheral neuropathy can be classified as (a) primarily sensory, which may exist in latent (detectable only by nerve conduction velocity measurements) or symptomatic form; (b) primarily motor with a division into latent and symptomatic, and (c) sensorimotor. Victor (1962) emphasizes the wide symptomatology ranging from cases with severe symptoms to asymptomatic cases found on routine examination. Sensory symptoms include burning sensation, pain and paraesthesia, and as with motor symptoms are more likely to affect the lower limbs before the upper limbs and the distal parts of the limb before the proximal. Pain may be constant or stabbing, and as with the burning sensation is either spontaneous or triggered off by contact, for example with bedclothes. The soles may be tender. Motor symptoms include weakness leading in severe cases to ankle and wrist drop. On examination, as expected, there is evidence of motor, sensory and reflex loss. The signs affect distal areas more than proximal and legs more than arms. The wasting is thus distal and also symmetrical as is the weakness and sensory loss, which involves all modalities. Deep tendon reflexes, particularly in the legs, are likely to be lost. Diagnostic tests include nerve conduction studies, and possibly abnormal low pyruvate levels in the serum, whilst the cerebrospinal fluid is usually normal. Rarely, alcoholic polyneuropathy may advance rapidly, mimicking infectious polyneuritis; in the latter, however, the cerebrospinal fluid protein level is usually clearly elevated. Withdrawal of alcohol and administration of vitamins may or may not bring about recovery, recovery usually being slow even in successfully-treated cases.

Alcoholic amblyopia refers to the loss of vision of gradual onset occurring in alcoholics with degeneration of the optic nerves and believed to be due to deficiency of vitamins of the B group. It is also said to be reversible in its early stages if alcohol and B vitamins are given.

Syndromes in which the aetiology is uncertain

These include cerebellar degeneration, Marchiafava—Bignami disease (primary degeneration of the corpus callosum) and central pontine myelinolysis. The former presents with ataxia of trunk and disturbance of balance and gait with minimal ataxia of limbs and speech disturbance in a middle-aged patient, often with evidence of malnutrition. It has to be distinguished from a similar syndrome in this age group, namely cerebellar degeneration in association with a primary carcinoma, of the bronchus for example. Marchiafava—Bignami disease was described first in wine drinkers and has been described in cases of malnutrition unassociated with alcoholism. A gradual degeneration of the corpus callosum and associated structures occurs. Clinically the patient presents with dementia accompanied by pains, dysesthesia and fits. Central pontine myelinolysis was first described by Adams, Victor and Mancall (1959) in two fatal cases presenting with quadriplegia and pseudobulbar palsy. At post mortem, a large area of demyelination in the centre of the pons was found.

MUSCULAR DISORDERS

These have been reviewed by Lees (1967) and may be acute with acute muscle necrosis resulting in pain, local tenderness and oedema and interference with renal function from the products of muscle breakdown, or chronic with involvement of proximal muscle groups and resulting weakness and tenderness. Perkoff *et al.* (1967) have examined these syndromes in detail. They showed that alcoholics in whom no muscular symptoms were present but who gave a history of cramps gave biochemical findings similar to symptomatic patients. A recent case report in Britain which overlapped both groups was that of O'Brien and Goldstraw (1969). They described a 46-year-old male with a long history of heavy drinking who presented with pectoral and pelvic girdle weakness (i.e. chronic syndrome) but whose biopsy showed changes of the acute syndrome as described by others. They state, 'It would appear that there is considerable overlap in the various syndromes.'

ACCIDENTS

The importance of alcohol as a factor in producing accidents whether at work, in the home and on the road has become evident from several studies. The importance of alcoholism as a factor in industrial accidents has been reviewed by Demone and Kasey (1966). They discuss the important American study of Observer and Maxwell (1959), who examined the records of a large American company. Such information gave details of all industrial injuries and accidents, illness absences of eight or more days' duration, and all 'off the job' accidents requiring time off. From these employees they took a group of 48 problem drinkers (32 males and 16 females) with a matched control group. The problem drinkers had two and a half times as many cases of illness or injury-caused absences (necessitating absences of at least eight days) compared with the control group, and in the below 40 years age group the 'on the job' accident rate was twice as great in the problem drinkers group. In the over-forties the 'on the job' accident rate was almost identical with the controls and they suggested that as people became older they realized their drinking problem and took protective measures to minimize accidents. Considering 'off the job' accidents, there were 21 cases requiring an absence of eight days or more in the problem drinkers and none at all in the controls. Combining both groups of accidents in men and women the problem drinker group had three to six times the rate of the control group.

The contribution that alcoholism makes to fatal non-traffic accidents has been estimated by Bertholdt (1967) in San Francisco. Examining accident deaths of 1343 alcoholics and comparing the fatal accident death rates from various causes of normal population, they found alcoholics were sixteen times as likely to die in an accidental fall and thirty times as likely to die from accidental poisoning. The contribution of alcohol to both attempted and actual suicide is discussed in the following chapter.

In relation to home accidents and the contribution alcohol makes, Kirkpatrick and Tanbenhaus (1967) looked at a random sample of 94 patients presenting with home accidents and measured blood alcohol levels. Seventeen out of 94 patients had a blood alcohol level above zero and in 11 the level was greater than 50 mg %. The bulk of injuries were lacerations. Wechsler *et al.* (1969) gave 'breathalysers' to 5622 patients attending a casualty department with a variety of injuries. Amongst these patients with home accidents producing injuries, 22.3 per cent had a positive breathalyser reading. Of patients involved in fights, 56.4 per cent had a positive breathalyser reading, whilst in 39 per cent of these the reading was 0.05% or more. Of patients admitted for non-accident reasons 8.9 per cent also had a positive breathalyser reading.

REFERENCES

Adams, R. D., Victor, M. and Mancall, E. L. (1959). 'Central pontine myelinolysis.' *Archs Neurol. Psychiat., Chicago* 81, 154

Bertholdt, B. (1967). 'Alcoholism and fatal accidents.' *Q. Jl Stud. Alcohol* 28, 517

Bingham, J. R. (1960). 'Precipitating factors in peptic ulcer.' *Can. med. Ass. J.* 83, 205

Blane, H. T., Overton, W. F. Jr. and Chafetz, M. E. (1963). 'Social factors in diagnosis of alcoholism.' *Q. Jl Stud. Alcohol* 26, 640

British Medical Journal. Editorial, 'Alcoholic cardiomyopathy.' *Br. med. J.* 2, 247

Bockus, H. L., Kalser, M. H., Ruth, J. L. A., Bogoch, A. L. and Stein, G. (1955). 'Clinical features of acute inflammation of the pancreas.' *Archs intern. Med.* 96, 308

Bogdanski, I. and Lindenaur, H. J. (1966). 'Post Alcoholic Hypoglycaemia.' *Med. Servs J. Can.* 22, 614

Burch, G. E., Harb, J. M., Colcolough, H. C. and Tsui, C. Y. (1971). 'The effects of prolonged consumption of beer, wine and ethanol on the myocardium of the mouse.' *Johns Hopkins med. J.* 129, 130

Clark, M. (1973). 'The metabolic effects of alcohol in man.' In *Recent advances in medicine*, 16th Ed. by D. N. Baron, N. Compston and A. M., Dawson, Edinburgh; Churchill Livingstone

Cogbill, C. L. and Taek-Song, K. (1970). 'Acute pancreatitis.' *Archs Surg., Lond.* 100, 673

Danesin, A. (1970). 'Epileptic seizures in chronic alcoholics.' *Electroenceph. clin. Neurophysiol* 28, 214

Demone, H. W., Jr. and Kasey, E. H. (1966). 'Alcohol and non-motor vehicle injuries.' *Publ. Hlth Rep., Wash.* 81, 585

Domzalski, C. A. and Wedge, B. M. (1948). 'Elevated serum amylase in alcoholics.' *Am. J. clin. Path.* 18, 43

Edwards, G., Hawker, A., Williamson, V. and Hensman, C. (1966). 'London's Skid Row.' *Lancet* 1, 249

Edwards, G., Fisher, M. K., Hawker, A. and Hensman, C. (1967a). 'Clients of Alcoholism Information Centres.' *Br. med. J.* 4, 346

Edwards, G., Hensman, C., Hawker, A. and Williamson, V. (1967b). 'Alcoholics Anonymous: the anatomy of a self help group.' *Social Psychiat. (Ger,)* 1, 195

Engeset, A., Lyrgren, T. and Idsoe, R. (1963). 'The incidence of peptic ulcer among alcohol abusers and non-abusers.' *Q. Jl Stud. Alcohol* 24, 622

Evans, W. (1964). 'Alcoholic myocardiopathy.' *Prog. cardiovasc. Dis.* 7, 151

Glatt, M. M. (1955). 'Alcohol and epilepsy.' *Br. med. J.* 2, 737

Green, J. R. (1965). 'The incidence of alcoholism in patients admitted to medical wards of a public hospital.' *Med. J. Aust.* 1, 465

Hagnell, O. and Wretmark, G. (1957). 'Peptic ulcer and alcoholism.' *J. Psychosom. Res.* 2, 35

Havard, J. D. J. (1963). 'Alcohol and road traffic.' London; British Medical Association

Hines, J. B. (1969). 'Reversible megaloblastic and sideroblastic marrow abnormalities in alcoholic patients.' *Br. J. Haemat.* 16, 87

Hore, B. D. (1973). 'Alcohol dependence and neuropsychiatric syndromes due to alcohol.' In *Recent advances in medicine*, 16th edn. Ed. by D. N. Baron, N. Compston and A. M. Dawson. Edinburgh; Churchill Livingstone

Hore, B. D. and Smith, E. (1975). 'Who goes to alcoholism treatment units.' *Br. J. Addict.* 70, 263

Howard, J. M. and Ehrlich, E. W. (1960). 'Aetiology of pancreatitis.' *Ann. Surg.* 135, 152

Isbell, H., Fraser, H. F., Wikler, A., Belleville, K. E. and Eisenman, A. J. (1955). 'An experimental study of the aetiology of "rum fits" and Delirium Tremens.' *Q. Jl Stud. Alcohol* 16, 1

Journal of Alcoholism (1972). Editorial, 'Alcohol-induced hypoglycaemia.' *J. Alcoholism* 2, 26

Kirkpatrick, J. R. and Tanbenhaus, L. J. (1967). 'Blood alcohol levels of home accident patients.' *Q. Jl Stud. Alcohol* 28, 734

The Lancet (1968). Editorial. 'Alcohol and the liver.' *Lancet,* 2, 670

The Lancet (1969). Editorial. 'Alcohol and the blood.' *Lancet,* 2, 675

Lees, F. (1967). 'Alcohol and the nervous system.' *Hosp. Med.* 2, 267

Lelbach, W. K. (1966). 'Leberschäden bei chronischem Alkoholismus.' *Acta hepato-splenol.* 13, 321

Lewis, J. G. and Chamberlain, D. A. (1963). 'Alcohol consumption and smoking habits in male patients with pulmonary tuberculosis.' *Br. J. prev. soc. Med.* 17, 149

Mawdsley, C. and Mayer, R. F. (1965). 'Nerve conduction in alcoholic polyneuritis.' *Brain* 88, 335

McCurdy, P. P., Pierce, L. E. and Rath, C. E. (1962). 'Abnormal bone marrow morphistology in acute alcoholism.' *N. Eng. J. Med.* 266, 505

McDonald, R. A. (1964). *Haemochromatosis and haemosiderosis.* Springfield, Illinois; Charles C. Thomas

McDonald, R. A. (1965). 'Haemochromatosis and cirrhosis in different geographic areas.' *Am. J. med. Sci.* **249**, 36

Melmed, R. N. (1967). 'Alcohol and the liver.' *Hosp. Med.* **2**, 297

Mendellson, J. M. (1964). 'Experimentally induced chronic intoxication and withdrawal in alcoholics.' *Q. Jl Stud. Alcohol* Suppl. 2

Morin, Y. (1966). 'Quebec's medical mystery.' *J. Am. med. Ass.* **197**, 592

Nolan, J. P. (1965). 'Alcoholism as a factor in the illness of university servia patients.' *Am. J. med. Sci.* **249**, 135

O'Brien, E. J. and Goldstraw, P. (1969). 'Alcoholic myopathy.' *Br. Med. J.* **4**, 785

Olin, J. S. and Grzybowski, S. (1966). 'Tuberculosis and alcoholism.' *Can. med. Ass. J.* **94**, 999

Observer and Maxwell, M. A. (1959). 'A study of absenteeism, accidents and sickness payments in problem drinkers in one industry.' *Q. Jl Stud. Alcohol* **20**, 302

Palmer, E. D. (1954) 'Gastritis–a revaluation.' *Medicine, Baltimore* **33**, 199

Pawar, P. B. (1972). 'Alcohol and hypoglycaemia.' *J. Alcoholism* **7**, 26

Paxton, J. R. and Payne, J. H. (1948). 'Acute pancreatitis.' *Surgery Gynec. Obstet.* **86**, 69

Pell, S. and D'Alonzo, C. A. (1968). 'The prevalance of chronic disease among problem drinkers.' *Archs envir. Hlth* **16**, 679

Perkoff, G. T., Dioso, M. M., Bleisch, V. and Klinkerfuss, G. (1967). 'A spectrum of myopathy associated with alcoholism I. Clinical and laboratory features.' *Ann. intern. Med.* **67**, 481

Phillips, G. B., Gabuzba, G. J., Jnr and Davidson, C. S. (1965). 'Cause of fatty cirrhosis in the alcoholic.' *J. clin. Invest.* **31**, 351

Pincock, T. A. (1964). 'Alcoholism in tuberculosis patients.' *Can. med. Ass. J.* **91**, 851

Pollock, A. V. (1959). 'Acute pancreatitis–analysis of 100 patients.' *Br. med. J.* **1**, 6

Powell, W. J. and Klatskin, G. (1968). 'Duration of survival in patients with Laennec's cirrhosis.' *Am. J. med.* **44**, 406

Retterstol, N. and Sund, A. (1962). 'Psychosomatic aspects of ulcus disease. Illustrated by material from psychiatric clinic.' *J. psychiat. Res.* **3**, 345

Rubin, E. and Lieber, C. S. (1968). 'Malnutrition and liver disease–an over-emphasized relationship.' *Am. J. Med.* **45**, 1

Sanders, M. (1970). 'Alcoholic cardiomyopathy–a critical review.' *Q. Jl Stud. Alcohol* **31**, 324

Smith-Moorhouse, P. M. and Lynn, L. (1969). 'Analysis of the work of an out-patients unit.' *Practitioner* **202**, 410

Strauss, R. and Bacon, S. D. (1951). 'Alcohol and social stability–a study of occupational integration in 2023 male clinic patients.' *Q. Jl Stud. Alcohol* **12**, 234

Sullivan, I. W. and Herbert, D. C. (1964). 'Suppression of haematopoesis by ethanol.' *J. clin. Invest.* **43**, 2048

Victor, M. (1971). 'Treatment of alcoholic intoxication and the withdrawal syndrome.' In *Treatment of the alcohol withdrawal syndrome*. Ed. by F. A. Seixas, New York, National Council on Alcoholism

Victor, M. (1962). 'Alcoholism.' In *Baker's Textbook of neurology*, Vol. **2**, Chap. 22. New York; Harper & Row

Victor, M. and Hope, J. M. (1958). 'The phenomenon of auditory hallucinations in chronic alcoholism.' *J. nerv. ment. Dis.* **126**, 451

Wechsler, H., Kasey, E. H., Thum, D. and Demone, J. H. W. (1969). 'Alcohol level and home accidents.' *Publ. Hlth Rep. Wash.* **84,** 1043

Weiner, H. A. and Tennant, M. P. (1938). 'A statistical study of acute haemorrhagic pancreatitis.' *Am. J. med. Sci.* **196,** 167

Wood, I. J. and Taft, L. I. (1958). 'Diffuse lesions of the stomach.' London; E. Arnold

Wynn Williams, A. (1956). 'Effects of alcohol on gastric mucosa.' *Br. med. J.* **1,** 256

Zieve, L. (1958). 'Jaundice: hyperlipaemia and haemolytic anaemia: a heretofore unrecognized syndrome associated with alcoholic fatty liver and cirrhosis.' *Ann. intern. Med.* **48,** 471

9

ALCOHOL INGESTION, ALCOHOLISM AND ROAD TRAFFIC ACCIDENTS

ALCOHOL INGESTION AND ROAD TRAFFIC ACCIDENTS

The importance of alcohol as a factor involved in road traffic accidents, both in relation to car drivers and pedestrians, has become of considerable interest in recent years. An important symposium was held in London in 1962 (Havard, 1963). Collister (1963) examined what people said about their drinking habits prior to a road traffic accident which led them to be admitted to one of four hospitals on the outskirts of London. Only 11 per cent admitted they had been drinking, but considering night accidents (10 p.m. to 4 a.m.) 36 per cent of drivers admitted to drinking alcohol, whilst in relation to day accidents only 6 per cent admitted involvement with alcohol. Fifty-two per cent of accidents in which alcohol was involved occurred on Saturday and Sunday. Collister reviewed previous studies in Britain. Earlier reports of subjective and objective opinions give lower rates of alcohol involvement than those with chemical analysis. In relation to the former, it is, of course, doubtful whether people will tell the truth; while, in relation to the latter, one notes the comment of Freeman (1964), who after describing the clinical effects of intoxication as of value to a police surgeon (slurred speech, full bounding pulse, smell of the breath, impaired memory, poor co-ordination, widely dilated pupils with little or no reaction to light and fine lateral nystagmus), adds that with the exception of the smell of the breath each and every symptom or sign can be explained by a cause other than alcohol.

Most important would appear to be those studies with chemical estimations of alcohol content of blood and/or urine. Thus Cassie and Allen (1961) examined 574 patients attending a hospital in Manchester following a road traffic accident and obtained a blood sample for alcohol estimation in 64 per cent of them. Amongst these patients blood alcohol levels were estimated and the results for accidents occurring at different times of the day are shown. In Table 2 are given the percentages of patients who had suffered a road traffic accident with different alcohol levels at various times whilst Table 3 describes the situation in relation to drivers only.

TABLE 2

Percentage of Road Traffic Accident Patients Arriving at Certain Times with 20, 50 and 100 mg % Blood Alcohol (Derived from Cassie and Allen, 1961)*

Blood alcohol	6–12 a.m.	12–6 p.m.	6–12 p.m.	12–6 a.m.
20	16.6	30.9	57.2	73.3
50	7.8	11.8	35.8	61.3
100	1	10.0	22.0	37.3

TABLE 3

Percentage of Road Traffic Accident Drivers Arriving at Certain Times with 20, 50 and 100 mg % Blood Alcohol (Derived from Cassie and Allen, 1961)*

Blood alcohol	6–12 a.m.	12–6 p.m.	6–12 p.m.	12–6 a.m.
20	17.1	36.8	53.5	64.5
50	0	10.5	33.3	58.3
100	0	7.0	22.2	31.2

* Reproduced with permission of *British Medical Journal*

Hopkinson and Widdowson (1964) estimated blood alcohol levels in 74 per cent of people involved in road traffic accidents. Considering the peak accident period (10 p. m. to 2 a.m.), 58 per cent of drivers had blood alcohol levels greater than 50 mg %. Watson (1961), cited by Collister (1963), investigated the urine alcohol and in some cases the blood alcohol levels in 139 road accident casualties admitted to the Royal Infirmary, Derby, during 1960. He found evidence of alcohol in 67 cases, i.e. 48 per cent of cases.

Haddon (1963) gives a comprehensive review of the subject. He discusses first the results of many experimental studies on driving performance. He states: 'The effects of alcohol on many psychological functions of importance in driving have been studied in the laboratory using human subjects, and most have been found to deteriorate at surprisingly low blood alcohol concentrations.' He describes different studies that consistently show that at least some important driving functions deteriorate at blood levels of 30–40 mg %.

Similar findings arise from epidemiological studies. Smith and Popham in Toronto (1951) compared blood alcohol concentrations amongst drivers involved in accidents in which the driver had been independently rated as highly responsible for the accident and those where the driver was rated not responsible or only slightly so. He demonstrated an increasing statistical excess of accidents which first became statistically significant in the 30–50 mg % range. Haddon (1963) quotes a further study in Toronto where it was shown that drivers who had a blood alcohol level of $\geqslant$ 150 mg % were eight times as common in an accident group compared with non-accident control groups obtained by stopping at each accident site 'four or more . . . drivers passing the scene . . . in cars of the same vintage'. Examining subjects involved in fatal car accidents in certain boroughs of New York City and comparing these subjects with a control group selected from a random sample of subjects stopped at the same time and same site as the accident, McCarrol and Haddon (1962) found the main difference was in relation to prior use of alcohol. Seventy-three per cent of individuals had been drinking prior to the accident whilst only 26 per cent of the control group had been drinking. Forty-six per cent of the accident-responsible group had blood alcohol concentrations greater than 250 mg %; this level was not present in any of the control subjects.

A study involving a similar technique but looking at pedestrians killed in motor vehicle accidents was also carried out by one of these authors (Haddon *et al.*, 1961). He and his co-workers looked at a series of 50 adult pedestrians fatally injured by road accidents in Manhattan and compared these with a group of matched controls obtained at the same sites, times of day and days of week. Seventy-four per cent of the pedestrians fatally injured had been drinking in comparison with 33 per cent of the control group.

It is perhaps with single motor vehicle accidents that the accident is most likely to be due to impaired performance of the driver. Haddon and Bradess (1959) examined blood alcohol levels (obtained at post mortem) in 83 out of 87 subjects who died within 4 hours of a fatal single vehicle accident. Forty-nine per cent of these had blood alcohol levels of 150 mg % or more. The authors consider that blood alcohol levels of this or greater magnitude are known to impair driving performance.

ALCOHOL INGESTION, ROAD TRAFFIC OFFENCES AND LEGISLATION

There has been considerable variation in legislation regarding drinking alcohol and driving and the manner in which possible offenders are dealt with. Bowden (1961) has reviewed this for many countries. In some countries medical (including biochemical) examination is compulsory in suspected cases, for example in Norway, Sweden and Denmark, whilst in some parts of the U.S.A. the interesting concept of 'implied consent' exists. This regards driving a vehicle as a privilege and not as a right. This privilege by the State is withdrawn if a person refuses to co-operate with examination. Punishment also varies in different countries from fines to a term of imprisonment. The B.M.A. Committee (1960), in assessing evidence, concluded that compulsory examination was of prime importance. An editorial in the *Journal of Forensic Medicine* (1964), which is highly critical of the B.M.A. report even in terms of accuracy, warns against this being regarded as a panacea. Indeed, some states, including Tennessee, claim that random testing by road blocks is the most important factor in reducing accidents. Bowden (1961) lists several ways in which road traffic accidents due to alcohol may be reduced. These include differential taxation of beverages (for example, the stronger the beverage the higher the taxation, as in Norway), education in schools such that driving after drinking is a social disgrace (this is said to have occurred in Medicine Hat in Alberta), prompt detection as by the use of large numbers of well-educated police, road blocks and compulsory examination, preferably by independent doctors and severe penalties for offenders as in Scandinavia. He strongly emphasizes that there is no simple answer and no country has yet found the ideal solution.

RELATIONSHIP BETWEEN ROAD TRAFFIC ACCIDENTS AND ALCOHOLISM

Earliest reports came from Sweden where in 1952 Bjerver, Goldberg and Linda found that alcohol misusers were overrepresented amongst subjects of road traffic accidents as compared with the general population. In Canada, Schmidt and Smart (1959) examined the accident records of all male patients admitted to an alcoholic unit in Ontario during a period of nine months. An attempt to show some measure of validity was made by looking at accidents and traffic offences incurred by such subjects in official records of the Ontario Department of Highways during the previous year. Alcoholic drivers compared with the general Ontario population were involved in significantly more accidents per year, and per mile driven, and were more often convicted for drunken and impaired driving.

In Eire, Clare and Cooney (1971) looked at 100 alcoholic car drivers and a control group in relation to prosecution for road traffic offences and frequency of road traffic accidents. The alcoholic group had four times as many of the former and twice as many of the latter.

Contributions from the U. S. A. include those of Bertholdt (1967), Selzer *et al.* (1963) and Selzer and Weiss (1966). Bertholdt in a study already mentioned found that alcoholics were 4½ times more likely to die in a motor vehicle accident than the expected rate. Selzer *et al.* (1963) examined 67 drivers arrested for drunken driving (7 female, 60 male) awaiting sentence. Thirty-eight of these (57 per cent) were considered to be alcoholics. In the second study (Selzer and Weiss, 1966) they looked at a group of drivers who had been responsible for 72 fatal accidents. Interviews were of these drivers (if surviving) and relatives if deceased. Considerable trouble was taken with these interviews; on an average in relation to each driver three interviews were made. Their definition of alcoholism was as follows: 'Alcoholism is a symptom of chronic emotional illness characterized by repeated drinking in amounts sufficient to cause injury to the driver's health or to his socio-economic functioning.' Of the 72 drivers, 40 per cent were considered to be alcoholics and 10 per cent problem drinkers. The title of this paper, 'Alcoholism and traffic fatalities—a study in futility', is perhaps a timely reminder of the great risk that is present when alcoholics are freely allowed to drive.

REFERENCES

Bertholdt, B. (1967). 'Alcohol and fatal accident.' *Q. Jl Stud. Alcohol* **28,** 517

Bjerver, K. B., Goldberg, L. and Linda, P. (1952). In *Proceedings 2nd. International Conference on Alcoholism and Road Traffic, Toronto,* p. 92

B. M. A. (1960). Special Report, 'Alcohol and road accidents.' *Br. med. J.* **1,** 269

Bowden, K. M. (1961). Report of the Senior Government Pathologist on Investigations Overseas with Detection of Drunken Driving, Melbourne. *J. forens. Med.* 9, 86 **10,** 111, 148; **11,** 6, 42; **12,** 93; **13,** 44

Cassie, A. B., and Allen, N. R. (1961). 'Alcohol and road traffic accidents.' *Br. med. J.* **2,** 1668

Clare, A. W. and Cooney, J. G. (1973). 'Alcoholism and road accidents.'*J. Ir. med. Ass.* **66,** 281

Collister, R. M. (1963). 'The incidence of alcohol and road traffic accidents.' In *Alcohol and road traffic*, Ed. by J. D. J Havard; London; British Medical Association

Freeman, S. (1964). 'The drinking driver.' *Br. med. J.* **2**, 1634

Havard, J. D. J. (Ed.) (1963). *Alcohol and road traffic*. London: British Medical Association

Haddon, W. J. and Bradess, V. A. (1959). 'Alcohol in the single vehicle fatal accident.' *J. Am. med. Ass.* **169**, 1587

Haddon, W., Jnr. (1963). 'Alcohol and highway accidents.' In *Alcohol and road traffic.* Ed. J. D. J. Havard, London: British Medical Association

Haddon, W., Jnr., Valien, P., McCarrol, T. R. and Umberger, C. J. (1961). 'A controlled investigation of the characteristics of adult pedestrians fatally injured by motor vehicles in Manhattan.' *J. chron. Dis.* **14**, 655

Hopkinson, B. R. and Widdowson, G. M. (1964). 'Relation of alcohol to accidents.' *Br. med. J.* **2**, 1569

Journal of Forensic Medicine (1964). Editorial, 'Alcohol and road accidents.' *J. forens. Med.* **2**, 89

McCarrol, J. R. and Haddon, W., Jnr. (1962). 'A controlled study of fatal automobile accidents in N. Y. county.' *J. chron. Dis.* **15**, 811

Schmidt, W. S. and Smart, R. G. (1959). 'Alcoholics, drinking and traffic accidents.' *Q. Jl Stud. Alcohol* **20**, 631

Selzer, M. L. and Weiss, S. (1966). 'Alcoholism and traffic fatalities—a study in futility.' *Am. J. Psychiat.* **122**, 762

Selzer, M. L., Payne, C. E., Gifford, J. D. and Kelly, W. C. (1963). 'Alcoholism, mental illness and the drunken driver.' *Am. J. Psychiat.* **120**, 326

Smith, H. W. and Popham, R. E. (1951). 'Blood alcohol levels in relation to drinking.' *Can. med. Ass. J.* **65**, 325

10

PSYCHIATRIC MORBIDITY

The principal neuropsychiatric syndromes associated with alcohol abuse are delirium tremens, Wernicke's encephalopathy, Korsakoff's syndrome, memory disturbances (apart from the latter syndrome) in the alcoholic, brain damage due to alcohol, alcoholic hallucinosis, morbid jealousy (the Othello syndrome), alcoholic fugue state, and the increased risk of suicide in the alcoholic.

DELIRIUM TREMENS

This is the most serious part of the alcohol withdrawal syndrome and in its full form is relatively uncommon (Victor, 1971). Victor analysed 266 consecutive patients admitted to Boston City Hospital with alcoholic complications and found only 5 per cent of these had typical delirium tremens. As the condition is part of a withdrawal syndrome it is likely to occur when alcohol intake ceases, as on being admitted to an environment free of alcohol such as a hospital or prison cell. The alcohol withdrawal syndrome has been described by Victor and Hope (1958) and Victor (1971). It has been emphasized by some authors that abstinence leading to the syndrome may not always be absolute but may be relative; the syndrome can occur despite an alcohol intake which is, however, lower than the usual regular intake. The withdrawal syndrome as described by Victor consists of tremulousness (combined with malaise, irritability, nausea and vomiting), hallucinosis, fits and delirium and has been produced experimentally by Isbell et al. (1955) and Mendellson (1964). Tremulousness usually reaches its peak 24 hours after cessation of intake whilst hallucinosis may begin then and extend for a week in the majority of cases. According to Victor, fits

79

occur mainly in the first two days. Tremulousness and fits have been considered in the previous chapter whilst alcoholic hallucinosis is described below.

Auditory hallucination (alcoholic hallucinosis) states may feature only to a minor extent in some forms of alcohol withdrawal syndromes. For this reason Knott and Beard (1971) state that the withdrawal syndromes may be divided into withdrawal of the delirium tremens type and of the alcoholic hallucinosis type. The former consists of hyperactivity, tremulousness and hallucinations (visual, tactile and auditory, delusions, confusion and fits).

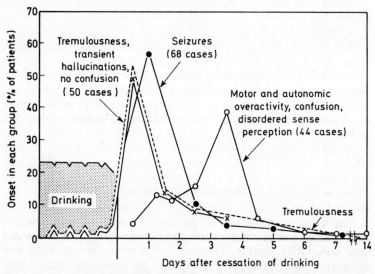

Figure 2. Data from hospitalized patients showing development of clinical symptoms of acute neurological disturbances following withdrawal of alcohol. The shaded area representing the period of drinking is greatly condensed. Successive low peaks in this area indicate tremulousness and nervousness that occur each morning after the night's abstinence. (From Victor, 1970; copyright McGraw–Hill Inc. Reprinted with permission)

Delirium tremens may occur in its full form or in less severe forms. These syndromes are forms of the acute organic reaction (toxic confusional state). Features of this include clouding of consciousness with disorientation in time and space, impaired grasp of reality, illusions, hallucinations, whether visual, tactile and auditory, the development of paranoid ideas, and delusions and misinterpretations. The patient is usually frightened, restless, tremulous and excitable. In severe cases fever, sweating and tachycardia may be marked. The aetiology of the syndrome in biochemical terms remains obscure but is considered below. The syndromes of delirium tremens (typical and atypical) usually last around 72 hours although cases may persist for weeks. Amnesia on recovery for events during the period is often complete or near-complete. In its full form delirium tremens is a serious condition. Victor (1971) reports that 15 per cent of his cases ended fatally. The majority of cases which carry a good prognosis are considered by him to be partial or less severe forms of the same disease. Death may be in association with infection, injury, hyperthermia, circulatory collapse or for no obvious reason.

The features of the alcohol withdrawal syndrome are shown graphically in *Figure 2*.

Gross and his colleagues have made several important contributions to this field. They have developed a quantitative rating scale (Gross, Lewis and Nagarajan, 1973) both reliable and valid to measure the alcohol withdrawal syndrome. Such a scale will be of considerable value in trials of agents used in the management of the syndrome, and also will permit cross cultural studies. Clinical impression suggests for example that the syndrome is less severe in Britain than in the U. S. A.

Further (Gross *et al.*, 1972), after a decade of research, they have subjected to a factor analysis data obtained from the systematic examination and recording of 100 patients undergoing acute alcohol withdrawal. Three factors emerged, accounting for 66 per cent of the observed clinical variation, and were independent. Factor I consisted of nausea, vomiting, tinnitus, visual disturbances, paraesthesia, muscle pain, pruritis, visual, auditory and tactile hallucinations, agitation and sleep disturbance. Factor II consisted of tremors, sweats, depression and anxiety and Factor III of clouding of the sensorium, altered states of consciousness, imparied control, nystagmus and disturbance of gait.

Mechanism of withdrawal syndrome

The mechanism of the withdrawal syndrome remains ill understood as of course does the biochemical mechanism of physical dependence on alcohol. Wolfe and Victor (1969) have emphasized the importance of a low serum magnesium level occurring during withdrawal which may relate to increased neuroexcitability and convulsions. Alcoholic patients on admission who showed photomyoclonus (on photic stimulation) had significantly lower serum magnesium levels than patients who did not. The former group (i.e. those who did show photomyoclonus) also were more likely to have spontaneous fits and delirium tremens. Photomyoclonus could also be eliminated by elevating serum magnesium levels with infusions of magnesium sulphate. In four patients in whom arterial pH and P_{CO_2} were measured and alkalaemia resulted, due probably to a respiratory alkalosis induced by hyperventilation. Both alkalosis and hypomagnesaemia were closely related in time and transient, returning to normal in 40–60 hours. They conclude: 'It is therefore postulated that hypomagnesaemia and alkalosis, each of which is known to be associated with hyperexcitability of the nervous system are compounded to produce photomyoclonus and spontaneous seizures and perhaps other symptoms that characterize the early phase of alcohol withdrawal.'

Mendellson, Ogata and Mello (1969), in carefully controlled experiments, found that in alcoholics during the first few days of withdrawal a significant fall in serum magnesium does occur and this coincides with the onset of neuromuscular hyperexcitability. It should also be noted that transient decrease in other serum electrolytes, particularly potassium, occurs. During the later stage of withdrawal, that is, by the fifth day, the serum magnesium has risen to normal levels. It should be noted that it is in the later part of the withdrawal period (third, fourth, fifth day) that the syndrome of delirium tremens occurs, although compared with controls they found delirium tremens patients as a group to have mean levels of serum magnesium lower than controls. There was not a one to one relationship as some patients with delirium tremens had normal serum levels. It would appear from these studies that whilst the increased neuroexcitability seen in the early withdrawal phase may be attributable to a low serum magnesium level and an alkalaemia, the contribution of these changes to the later stages of the withdrawal syndrome (i.e. delirium tremens) remains less clear. Recent theories on the aetiology of alcohol dependence and its possible link to biogenic amine metabolism have been considered in Chapter 6.

Management

This has been the subject of a recent review (Seixas, 1971). Victor (1971) has emphasized that a search for an associated injury and infection should be made and that correction of fluid defect and electrolyte imbalance is the cornerstone of management. Tavel, Davidson and Batterton (1961) examined 39 fatalities from delirium tremens occurring in a nine year period. Thirty-six patients died during the phase of delirium. Principal clinical features including pulmonary complications (21 cases), hyperthermia of 104 °F (40 °C) or more

(20 cases), enlarged liver (19 cases), renal hypertension (19 cases), trauma (13 cases), malnutrition (13 cases), dehydration (12 cases) and convulsions (12 cases). The common fatal sequence would appear to be hyperthermia, dehydration, hypovolaemia leading to circulatory collapse together with abnormal pulmonary and hepatic functioning. Circulatory collapse and hyperthermia if present will require treatment in their own right. Nursing in a side room with constant nursing personnel is desirable, as with other confusional states (Hore, 1972).

Sedative Drugs

A wide range of sedatives including phenothiazines, particularly chlor-promazine (Largactil) chlordiazepoxide (Librium), chlormethiazole edisylate (Heminevrin), paraldehyde, doxepin (Sinequan), barbiturates and hydroxyzine (Vistaril), have been recommended. In addition the use of vitamins, especially thiamine, and glucose given intravenously have been emphasized by some. Although chlorpromazine is probably the drug most frequently used in Britain it has been criticized in that it may induce fits and hypotension and is not cross tolerant with alcohol as are chlordiazepoxide and paraldehyde (Edwards, 1967). In a double-blind controlled comparison of chlordiazepoxide, chlorpromazine, hydroxyzine, thiamine and a placebo in 539 patients suffering acute withdrawal symptoms, Kaim, Klett and Rothfield (1971) found fits developed least in the chlordiazepoxide group (1 per cent) and most (12 per cent) in the chlorpromazine group. In the cases treated by the former drug only 1 per cent developed delirium tremens and the chlorpromazine group had the highest incidence of delirium tremens (7 per cent). They concluded that although there was no consistent overall superiority of any one treatment chlordiazepoxide was the drug of choice. Sereny and Kalant (1965) carried out a double-blind trial of 58 male alcoholics aged 28—54 comparing chlordiazepoxide in two doses, promazine in two doses and a placebo. The aims were to assess the various combinations in two ways: firstly, the degree to which they improve well-being and secondly, the degree to which they prevent serious complications such as fits. In relation to the former, although both promazine and chlordiazepoxide reduced sleeplessness and sweating the effect of the former rapidly wore off as patients became tolerant. Tremor on the other hand increased with chlordiazepoxide; in relation to prevention of fits, numbers were too small for assessment. However, no patient developed fits on chlor-diazepoxide, whereas five did on promazine.

Victor (1971) considers paraldehyde to be the most effective drug in both severe and milder cases and it has the advantage of being safe and non-toxic. He believes however that there is no evidence that *any* drug shortens the duration or reduces mortality of the full form of delirium tremens.

It is clear that there remains considerable argument as to the drug of choice. Probably chlorpromazine, chlordiazepoxide, paraldehyde and in Britain chlormethiazole are the drugs most frequently used. It should be emphasized that the aim of sedation should not be to render the patient deeply unconscious but to diminish in severity the confusion, hallucinations, fear, etc. The drug is given in decreasing doses for 7–10 days and then stopped. Chlormethiazole has been used in Britain (Glatt and Frisch, 1969) in a double-blind trial (chlormethiazole and a placebo) in a group of alcoholics during the withdrawal phase. Patients in the chlormethiazole group showed significantly more rapid improvement than those in the placebo group. Harfast, Greene and Lasalle (1967) found, however that chlormethiazole was not superior to a barbiturate in relieving withdrawal symptoms. The author has found chlormethiazole to be a useful drug in the following regime: days 1, 2, 3–3 tabs of 500 mg q.d.s.; days 4, 5, 6–2 tabs of 500 mg q.d.s.; days 7, 8, 9–1 tab of 500 mg q.d.s. It should be added that some authorities (Glatt, personal communication, 1974) consider it should be given for only 6 days in order to minimize problems of dependence. However, the author has not found any problem of dependence using the above regime.

Other drugs

Use of vitamins, particularly vitamins of the B group, and anticonvulsants has been recommended (Knott and Beard, 1971; Bissl, 1971). Knott and Beard (1971) and Bissl (1971) recommend B vitamins as part of routine management. Victor (1971), however, in discussing vitamins in the light of the absence of controlled studies concludes: 'Our studies have convinved us that nutritional factors are not of prime importance in the causation of delirium tremens and that these disorders subside in a natural matter despite the lack of all food and vitamins.'

Knott and Beard (1971) recommend the routine use of anticonvulsants such as diphenylhydantoin in decreasing dosage for 2–3 weeks as an attempt to restore the electrical gradients across cell membranes produced by the effect of alcohol on the cell membrane, the effect being an increase in intracellular sodium concentration and a   decrease in intracellular potassium. Such shifts may underlie the increased excitability of nervous tissue and increase the likelihood of fits. Diphenylhydantoin is believed to affect cell membranes in such a way as to restore the original $Na^+ : K^+$ ratio. Bissl (1971) suggests, however, that very large doses of diphenylhydantoin would have to be given for an anticonvulsant effect to occur. Victor (1971) also points out that fits are likely to occur early in the withdrawal phase of alcohol and that they are likely to be over before drugs such as diphenyl-hydantoin become effective. Magnesium sulphate as a source of magnesium (Mg^{2+}) has also been recommended to replace depleted magnesium, said to occur in alcoholics, and in theory restore magnesium levels to normal and reduce neural excitability (Knott and Beard, 1971; Bissl, 1971).

Alcohol may reduce blood sugar levels as stated in a previous chapter, probably by depleting glycogen stores in the liver and interfering with glucogenesis. It would seem reasonable to use 50 ml of 50% glucose intravenously as part of routine management of the withdrawal syndrome.

Summary

Although some aspects of the management of typical and atypical cases of delirium tremens remain controversial there is sufficient agreement regarding the following. Although the majority of cases are minor in severity, the condition is a potentially serious one and may require all the resources of a medical unit. For this reason the author believes that ideally such cases should be managed on a medical ward. Awareness of such complications as electrolyte disturbance, circulatory collapse and hyperthermia is essential and careful monitoring of the patient required. Nursing in a quiet environment with a minimum of change of nursing personnel and minimal fuss is recommended. As regards sedation it is important to re-emphasize that the aim of this is to reduce the severity of confusion, fits, etc. and not to comatose the patient. As regards choice of sedative, paraldehyde, chlordiazepoxide, chlormethiazole and chlorpromazine all have adherents. The latter does, however, have the risk of increasing the likelihood of fits and hypotension. The routine use of anticonvulsants, vitamins and hypoglycaemia has not been accepted by all.

WERNICKE'S ENCEPHALOPATHY/KORSAKOFF'S PSYCHOSIS

An outstanding account of large series of cases of these syndromes has been given by Victor (1962), who also gives extracts from their original descriptions. The two syndromes appear to be closely related. Thus Victor (1962) found the majority of his patients with Korsakoff's psychoses showed evidence of the stigmata of Wernicke's encephalopathy even years later; conversely patients with Wernicke's encephalopathy may show a mental state similar to Korsakoff's psychoses. Further cerebral lesions may be identical whether the patient dies in the Wernicke's form or Korsakoff's form of the disease.

Wernicke's encephalopathy

This was described in 1881 by Wernicke as an acute illness of sudden onset characterized by a triad of mental confusion, paralysis of ocular movement and ataxia of gait. All the original three patients died and Victor states that a fatal outcome was regarded as usual.

Post-mortem examination of fatal cases reveals lesions to be wider than originally believed, affecting grey matter and the third and fourth ventricles and Sylvian aqueduct; that is, involving the thalamus, hypothalamus, mid-brain, floor of fourth ventricle and mammillary bodies, lesions here being most constant. Microscopically the lesions indicate cell necrosis.

Clinical features

A very large series has been reported by Victor (1962) who describes 200 cases seen in Boston. The principal features were firstly, ocular signs; secondly, ataxia of gait, and thirdly, abnormal mental states. Onset was usually acute, the former two features preceding the latter by days and weeks. The former include nystagmus of both horizontal and vertical type, paralysis of lateral recti and paralysis of convergent gaze. Victor states that paralysis of downward gaze is a very uncommon manifestation. Ataxia of gait and stance of varying degrees ranging from inability to stand and walk, to examples evident only on special tests, such as heel—shin co-ordination, was a feature of the above series whilst dysarthria was rare, as was ataxia of upper limbs. Abnormal mental states were present in 90 per cent of Victor's cases and were of three types: an acute confusional state, a Korsakoff state and a group in which the predominant features were apathy, listlessness, inability to concentrate and attend, the latter making formal mental testing very difficult. In addition to the triad of symptoms above, peripheral neuropathy of varying severity was present in over half of the cases.

Korsakoff's psychosis

This syndrome was described in 1889 by the Russian, S. S. Korsakoff. He drew attention to mental symptoms accompanying alcoholic peripheral neuropathy. Later he emphasized that the latter symptoms may be minimal. The principal features of the mental state are considered usually to be severe amnesia together with confabulation. However, Victor (1962) has emphasized that the initial mental state may be that of confusion and it is only when this has subsided that psychiatric testing shows abnormalities which indicate widespread intellectual impairment not confined to disturbance of memory. It is true, however, that memory impairment is the most marked of the intellectual defects. It usually takes the form of inability to learn new material and the inability to remember past events in their correct chronological sequence.

Victor, Herman and White (1957) administered the Weschler–Bellvue Intelligence Scale and Weschler Memory Scale to a group of fifteen patients suffering from the Wernicke–Korsakoff syndrome secondary to alcoholism. The principal results were as follows. Firstly, memory functions were the most clearly affected. The most marked defect was impaired capacity for learning new associations and for retention of newly-presented information such as short stories. In general, mental test abnormalities changed as the condition became more chronic. In the acute stage disorganization of mental functions may be so acute that the patient cannot participate in any formal tests. Later although cognitive impairment was widespread it was most marked in tests of memory. The relative degree of deterioration in different cognitive functions changed with progress of the condition, preventing a stable profile of intellectual impairment emerging from the disease. Ryback (1971), in a general review of memory disturbance in alcoholics, considers the memory defect in the Wernicke–Korsakoff syndrome to lie in short-term memory (memory for events which last 1–2 minutes or more, such as short stories) and in remote memory whilst immediate memory (events lasting from a few seconds to a minute) is relatively unimpaired.

Victor (1962) has discussed how the presence of confabulation is associated with two particular aspects of the mental state. During the confusional episode confabulation may arise from disordered perception and be akin to confabulation in other confusional states. During the later stages confabulation may depend on the patient's inability to remember events in their correct temporal order.

As regards outcome Victor (1962) considers that only a minority of patients fully recover although some degree of recovery (which may take months) may be expected in many patients with a decrease in confabulation as time passes and a slow improvement in relative memory, and in relating events in their correct chronological sequence.

Aetiology of the Wernicke/Korsakoff syndrome

It appears to be accepted by most authorities that at least in part these syndromes have their origin in deficiency of thiamine due to the associated nutritional deficiency seen in alcoholics. The relative lack in Britain of cases of these syndromes in recent years may lie in the better nutritional state of alcoholics afforded by the 'safety net' of the Welfare State. Wernicke's encephalopathy may occur in other states associated with vitamin deficiency such as repeated vomiting in hyperemesis gravidarum and experimentally-induced thiamine deficiency in animals may produce pathological brain lesions similar to those found in patients dying from the disease. Administration of thiamine to humans with Wernicke's disease may produce rapid resolution of ophthalmoplegia although mild forms of nystagmus and loco-motor ataxia may persist for much longer, even years. In relation to the mental states of Wernicke's encephalopathy Victor (1962) has emphasized that whilst apathy, listlessness, inability to concentrate and attend, respond to thiamine, the Korsakoff type of disturbance rarely does. He concludes this indicates this disturbance is due to structural (non-reversible) damage. Victor (1962) considers that whilst the confusional defect seen in the early stages of Korsakoff's psychosis may improve following thiamine administration, memory defect and confabulation recover slowly and incompletely. He concludes that whilst the ophthalmoplegia of Wernicke's syndrome and the early mental stages of Korsakoff's disease are likely to have a biochemical origin the memory defect and confabulation are more likely to be the result of structural lesions.

MEMORY DISTURBANCE IN THE ALCOHOLIC

Apart from the memory disturbances outlined in the previous section, among the early symptoms associated with excessive drinking are disturbances of memory (palimpsests). They may begin as amnestic periods covering the events surrounding the previous night's drinking, including such details as to how the patient finally arrived home. Later these episodes may lengthen such that memory may be impaired during periods of several days ('lost weekends'). During this period the patient may to observers appear to be fully in contact with his sur-roundings and carrying out everyday tasks. Ryback (1971) has recently reviewed memory disturbance in alcoholics. These disturbances can be produced experimentally in alcoholics and normal subjects by alcohol ingestion leading to a rapid rise in blood alcohol. It is during this phase of a rapidly-rising blood alcohol level that amnesias occur; once a high plateau level is maintained (200—250 mg %) then such amnesias do not develop. It would appear that short-term memory (i.e. memory for stimuli lasting 1—2 minutes or more) is primarily disrupted whilst immediate memory (i.e. memory stimuli lasting for a few seconds to a minute) and remote memory (recall of past events) remain intact. Such effects on memory function cannot be explained by hypoglycaemia. The clinical observation that the commonest memory disturbance is that of morning amnesias (inability to recall events surrounding the previous night's drinking, fits these data well in that because of the licensing laws in Britain the evening is the time *par excellence* when the abnormal drinker (who is most frequently of the 'loss of control' type) will ingest large quantities of alcohol, and there will be a rapidly-rising blood alcohol level. It is also of interest that Stein, Wiles and Ludwig (1968) found that the acute type of alcoholic amnesia occurred most commonly with the 'loss of control' type of drinking pattern.

Goodwin and his colleagues have also carefully examined memory disturbance in the alcoholic (Goodwin *et al.*, 1970, 1973; Goodwin and Hill, 1973).

In the earliest of these studies alcoholics were given high doses of alcohol whilst memory function and blood levels were monitored. Even with high levels (200—300 mg %), only subjects with a history of frequent 'blackouts' experienced short-term memory loss (defined as inability to remember events for thirty minutes). Goodwin and Hill (1973), in reviewing other studies, concluded that it was short-term memory loss rather than immediate loss (inability to remember events for one minute) that was affected, and this type of memory was based on retrieval or retention rather than registration. Goodwin *et al.* (1973) considered in a further study that this short-term memory defect was a 'threshold' rather than a 'graded' phenomenon.

Jonnson, Cronholm and Izikowitz (1962) and Claeson and Carlson (1970) have shown that intellectual impairment over a wide range of tests is evident after a short period of abstinence but that these changes may be reversible on continued abstinence.

BRAIN DAMAGE DUE TO ALCOHOL (ALCOHOLIC DEMENTIA)

The incidence of brain damage in alcoholic populations has remained unknown until recently although a relationship has long been suspected.

One difficulty has been the lack of precise criteria of brain damage. Psychometric tests have, despite the concept of 'verbal performance discrepancy', the disadvantage that in the absence of a previous test result with which the present results can be compared it is difficult to be certain that progressive changes have occurred. Electroencephalography (EEG) studies suggest that unless damage is gross the EEG may be normal.

The most precise method of assessing brain damage would appear to be that of the air encephalogram. As yet only a minority of reports have appeared using this test for reasonable numbers of alcoholics (Tumarkin, Malls and Baker, 1955; Skillicorn, 1955; Ferrer, 1970; Brewer and Perrett, 1971). Such studies are, however, of considerable importance as they represent the assessment of brain damage in alcoholic populations using a precise test. Brewer and Perrett (1971) examined 33 patients with a diagnosis of chronic alcoholism using psychometric testing, EEG studies and air encephalography. Seventy per cent of their patients showed radiologically-significant atrophy although in only 58 per cent of cases did psychometric testing lead to the diagnosis of significant brain damage. The most important radiological feature of atrophy was cortical atrophy. Both frontal and parietal areas were affected although the former were most commonly involved. EEG studies suggested this tool was of little value in assessing damage. It was considered that the high incidence of damage could not be accounted for by age and dietary deficiency. It should be noted that only one patient showed clinical evidence of brain damage and the majority of patients were not of the 'Skid Row' type. Ferrer (1955) in Chile found similar results for 56 demented alcoholics, particularly in the high incidence of frontal lobe cortical atrophy and in his view alcohol abuse rather than malnutrition was the major aetiological factor.

ALCOHOLIC HALLUCINOSIS

The awareness of a syndrome, occurring in subjects who abuse alcohol, consisting predominantly of auditory hallucinations has been known for many years. There has, however, been controversy as to whether such a syndrome is a form of schizophrenia or should be regarded as an independent example of organic brain disease. In recent years two important studies, those of Victor and Hope (1958) and Benedetti (1952), have clarified this conflict. Victor and Hope examined 70 alcoholic patients whose presentation was of an illness in which the clinical feature was the presence of auditory hallucinations in clear consciousness. Four of the patients had repeated attacks so that 76 episodes of alcoholic hallucinosis were observed and studied. These patients were part of 1037 patients examined in a study of alcoholism. Of 266 consecutive alcoholic admissions 16 patients (6 per cent) had auditory hallucinations. To examine the frequency of auditory hallucinations in a group of consecutive alcoholic admissions with hallucinations of various types, they looked at 50 such cases. Twenty-nine cases of this group (58 per cent) had purely visual hallucinations, 8 cases (16 per cent) purely auditory whilst 13 cases (26 per cent) had a mixed pattern.

In comparison with other complications of alcoholism in a large series of patients they concluded that the frequency of alcoholic hallucinosis (an illness characterized mainly by the presence of auditory hallucinations) was approximately that of delirium tremens, half as frequent as epilepsy and one sixth as frequent as the tremulousness seen in alcoholics.

Examining the 76 cases outlined above, which included full-blown cases of delirium tremens (in which auditory hallucinations were part of a wide range of perceptual abnormalities), in 23 cases the clinical feature was auditory hallucinations alone, in 11 cases these were accompanied by visual hallucinations, and in a further 11 both types of hallucination were accompanied with tremulousness. In 19 cases hallucinations of both types were accompanied by delusions (not derived from hallucinations) and fits. The mean age of male patients ($n = 56$) was 41 years whilst for female patients ($n = 14$) mean age was 38.3 years. In considering the relationship to schizophrenia of this syndrome an assessment of pre-recorded personality types is important. In the 31 patients they were able with confidence to assess to a personality type, 28 being regarded as cyclothymic and 3 as schizothymes. In considering other diagnosis in their subjects there were three patients who developed a schizophrenic illness prior to the onset of an auditory hallucinatory state associated with alcoholism. The authors explain that such patients must clearly be distinguished from those cases where there is no antecedent history of schizophrenia in which the illness begins as an acute alcoholic hallucinosis and later becomes chronic, resembling schizophrenia.

In relation to previous patterns of drinking 22 were 'spree' drinkers, whilst 35 were 'steady' drinkers and 5 showed a mixed pattern, 11 patients consumed whisky only, 8 ale only and 15 both whisky and ale. These were the three major groups of beverages.

If one accepts alcoholic hallucinosis as a form of schizophrenia one might expect a family history of this disorder to be present to a significantly greater degree than in a normal population. Unfortunately in this study for only 18 patients was there a systematic history obtainable. In only one of these cases was there a definite positive family history of schizophrenia.

The content of the hallucinations consisted in the vast majority of cases of voices. In 9 subjects non-vocal hallucinations were heard (buzzing, car motors, music, dogs barking, ringing) but in only 2 of these were these the only auditory phenomenon. The content of the vocal hallucinations was unpleasant and pleasant to an approximately equal degree (25 subjects in the former category and 20 in the latter).

Again in relationship to schizophrenia it is important to note that unlike earlier writers Victor and Hope did not find the majority of vocal hallucinations to be of the 'third person type'. Behaviour to these hallucinations was appropriate in all but a minority of cases which are considered below. The duration of hallucinations in 75 cases was less than one day (14 cases), 1–6 days (50 cases), 10–25 days (3 cases) and six weeks to five years (8 episodes). In the vast majority of cases therefore auditory hallucinations were relatively short-lived phenomena.

The eight patients whose hallucinations were prolonged represented an important sub-group in that after a few days' experiencing acute hallucinations and exhibiting appropriate behaviour to these as with other cases, they appeared to become resigned to their hallucinations and appeared unperturbed (behaviour thought to be inappropriate as the hallucinations were persisting). In addition they showed paranoid delusions, not all of which could be accounted for by the hallucinations. It should be noted that no obvious features other than clinical separated this group from the other.

As to the aetiology of the syndrome of alcoholic hallucinosis, two factors were considered of major importance, these being prolonged drinking and abstinence. The authors recorded that in 61 cases after heavy drinking hallucinations began following the last drink whilst in 15 cases the patients were still drinking. In 53 patients the actual time of the last drink was determined and in 32 of these (60 per cent) the onset occurred between 12–48 hours following withdrawal of alcohol, whilst in the remainder it began later, in some as long as a week. The authors consider the syndrome to be primarily a withdrawal syndrome which occurs earlier than that of delirium tremens. To account for the 15 cases who were drinking at the time the hallucinations began they consider the concept of relative abstinence, that is, withdrawal syndromes may occur despite the lack of total abstinence if there is a reduction in intake. However, they admit that they could not assess this factor accurately from the histories they had. As regards eventual outcome, 43 cases were contacted 4–5 years later and of these 3 were chronic subject hallucinators. There are similarities to theses cases in the report of Benedetti (1952), who reported on 113 cases. In the vast majority (90 out of 113) the syndrome was acute (hours, days or maximally a few days or months) with full recovery. Chronic forms of the hallucinosis have a different prognosis and end in cases resembling either schizophrenia or dementia. The acute form of alcoholic hallucinosis was often accompanied by organic features such as memory disturbance (mild) and delirium. Hallucinosis was linked with delirium in about 25 per cent of cases of acute hallucinosis. Considering the relationship to schizophrenia of the acute and chronic forms of alcoholic hallucinosis, Benedetti noted that the family background in acute cases was different from that found for schizophrenia in that relatives were much less frequently schizophrenic than relatives of schizophrenics. Although the incidence of schizophrenia in relatives was higher in the chronic group than the acute group, the number of chronic cases was really too small for definite conclusions to be reached.

Conclusions

Considering the results of these two major studies it would appear that in the majority of cases alcoholic hallucinosis is acute and the hallucinations disappear in a few days. Only a small minority of cases become chronic and it is these cases which resemble schizophrenia and may well be indistinguishable. Benedetti also considered that some cases become demented. These schizophrenic cases cannot on the limited evidence available be attributed to alcohol 'releasing' a schizophrenic illness in genetically-prone individuals. Both authors emphasize how acute alcoholic hallucinosis may occur in association with 'organic' features and Victor and Hope (1958) consider the syndrome to represent an early part of the withdrawal syndrome of alcohol dependence. The weight of evidence would support this view although how in a minority of cases changes then ensue to produce a schizophrenic-type illness remains a mystery.

Management of alcoholic hallucinosis

Admission to hospital is essential as it is frequently the only way of being certain that the patient remains free of alcohol intake. Hallucinations may subside spontaneously within a few days. If this does not occur it is advisable that phenothiazines, such as trifluoperazine (10 mg t.d.s.), are administered. The patient must be advised of the seriousness of his condition and total abstinence recommended and the patient advised to embark on an alcoholic rehabilitation programme.

MORBID JEALOUSY (OTHELLO SYNDROME)

This syndrome is reviewed by Enoch, Trethowan and Barker (1967). Alcoholism is only one of the conditions in which it may appear. In addition, the syndrome may rarely occur in a pure form. Enoch and co-workers consider the term *Othello syndrome* applicable to these cases only if the syndrome dominates all other features. The essential feature of the syndrome is the delusion of infidelity. The subject becomes convinced of his spouse or cohabitee's infidelity and the sexual partner is regularly harangued with accusations, denial not being accepted. Attempts to prove the partner's infidelity are constantly being made. This may involve the searching of possessions for incriminating evidence, such as tickets, hotel bills, etc., searching of underclothing and sheets for removal of stains, etc., frequent visits at unexpected hours to the house to catch the partner unawares, and attempts to follow the partner. Misinterpretations of events understandable in the light of the delusion may occur, for example, a change in the order of the home indicates 'someone' has been there. Sexual demands on the partner may increase and repulsion is strongly resented. Enoch, Trethowan and Barker (1967) point out that despite the efforts made above the patient rarely names the 'lover' and at times appears to avoid attempts to attain unequivocal proof. Such behaviour as mentioned above leads to progressive quarrelling and bitterness and sometimes to violence (Shepherd, 1961). Besides alcoholism, morbid jealousy occurs in paranoid states, epilepsy, dementia, manic–depressive psychoses and psychopathy (Enoch, Trethowan and Barker, 1967).

In relation to the aetiology of morbid jealousy it has been seen as an index of inferiority with projection of this 'inadequacy' onto the wife, who becomes 'bad' and 'inferior'. In relation to alcoholism there may be several factors predisposing to the condition: firstly, impotence, which is common and must appear as a 'threat' to the ego; secondly, the estrangement which occurs as a result of the alcoholic's behaviour and the wife's revulsion towards intercourse. This latter effect is interpreted as a lack of desire on her part which must mean she is receiving sexual satisfaction elsewhere.

ALCOHOLIC FUGUE STATE

Alcoholism is one of the well-recognized causes of fugue states, and as a cause has to be distinguished from other causes, notably hysterical fugues, depressive fugues and post-epileptic fugues. Fugues refer to those states where a patient wanders away from familiar surrounds and reappears in unfamiliar surroundings with amnesia for the intervening period. Alcoholic fugue states occur during a drinking bout and probably have as their basis the acute disturbance of memory induced by alcohol ingestion. To an onlooker the behaviour of the subject during the fugue may appear normal and rational. The patient, however, is amnestic for events during the period. Hysterical fugues can sometimes be distinguished by the relatively 'cared for' appearance of the subject compared with the alcoholic and, of course, by the negatives history of alcoholism. Such a history also clearly aids diagnosis from depressive and post-epileptic fugues.

ALCOHOL, ALCOHOL DEPENDENCE AND SUICIDE

Alcohol plays two distinct roles in relation to suicide. Firstly, many suicidal acts are committed following ingestion of alcohol; secondly, alcohol-dependent subjects have a much higher rate of suicide than non-alcohol-dependent subjects.

Glatt (1954) reviewed 22 alcoholics who had attempted suicide; 12 had done so below the age of forty; the majority of these were also regarded as psychopathic personalities. Batchelor (1954) reviewed 200 patients (92 male, 108 female) who had attempted suicide and been admitted to a general hospital in Edinburgh during the period 1950–1952. It was found that 32.6 per cent of the male patients and 12.1 per cent of the female gave histories of repeated excessive drinking although 19 of the total number of patients were also considered to be psychopathic and 15 depressives. Only 5 patients were considered to be chronic alcoholics. Of patients who drank excessively 46.5 per cent were not under the influence of drink at the time they attempted suicide. In his conclusion Batchelor considers alcoholism may influence suicidal acts in the following ways. A quarter of the patients came from homes broken because of parental alcoholism, and this 'broken home' may be a factor in shaping personality rendering the subject more likely to attempt suicide at a later date. Secondly, 'In the adult, alcoholism may prepare the way for suicide by hastening personal disintegration, material ruin and social estrangement.' Thirdly, the disinhibiting effect of alcohol may permit acts which would normally have been controlled.

He also points out that alcoholism may render suicidal acts less effective in rendering performance less competent, by reducing painful conflicts and that prolonged drinking may be seen as a less urgent prolonged form of suicide.

A more recent study producing a more definite link between alcoholism and suicide was that of Kessel and Grossman (1961). Prior to this Robins *et al.* (1959) in the U.S.A. had reviewed a consecutive series of 134 suicides and of the 119 for whom they had obtained adequate histories 31 were chronic alcoholics. Kessel and Grossman (1961) examined two series of chronic alcoholics. Firstly, 131 consecutive patients (110 males, 21 females) discharged from the Maudsley Hospital with a diagnosis of alcohol addiction were followed up for periods of between 12 months and 11 years (mean being 5.5 years). Secondly, 87 patients (62 males, 25 females) admitted to an acute psychiatric observation unit in London (St. Pancras) were followed up for between 4 and 5 years. Follow-up of the latter group was obtained by analysis of death registers held by the General Register Office (deaths in Scotland, Northern Ireland and other countries would be missed). The data on the bulk of the Maudsley patients were known to the clinicians who had looked after these patients.

Of the men, 9 (8 per cent) of the Maudsley series and 4 (7 per cent) of the St. Pancras series had killed themselves. This was 75–85 times the expected figure for males of these ages in Greater London calculated from the Registrar-General's (1960) report. None of the women in either series had committed suicide.

REFERENCES

Batchelor, I. R. C. (1954). 'Alcoholism and attempted suicide.' *J. ment. Sci.* **100,** 451

Benedetti, G. (1952). *Die alkoholhalluzinosen.* Stuttgart; Thieme. (English translation of summary available from Library, Institute of Psychiatry, London)

Bissl, L. C. (1971). 'Guidelines to management of alcohol withdrawal. In *Treatment of the alcohol withdrawal syndrome.* Ed. by F. A. Seixas, National Council on Alcoholism New York

Brewer, C. and Perrett, L. (1971). 'Brain damage, due to alcohol consumption–an air-encephalographic, psychometric and electroencephalographic study.' *Br. J. Addict.* **66,** 170

Claeson, L. E. and Carlson, C. (1970). 'Cerebral dysfunction in alcoholics.' *Q. Jl Stud. Alcohol* **31,** 317

Edwards, G. (1967). 'The meaning and treatment of alcohol dependence.' *Hosp. Med.* **2,** 272

Enoch, M. O., Trethowan, W. H. and Barker, J. C. (1967). 'Some uncommon psychiatric syndromes.' Bristol; J. Wright

Ferrer, S. (1970). *Complicaciones neurologicas cronicas del alcoholism.* Santiago, Chile; Editorial Universitaria

Glatt, M. (1954). Letter to the Editor 'Alcoholism and attempted suicide.' *Br. med. J.* **2,** 991

Glatt, M. and Frisch, P. (1969). 'Chlormethizole in alcoholism.' *Curr. psychiat. Ther.* **9,** 132

Goodwin, D. W., Otimer, E., Halikas, J. A. and Freeman, F. (1970). 'Loss of short term memory as a predictor of the alcoholic blackout.' *Nature, Lond.* **227,** 201

Goodwin, D. W., Hill, S. Y., Powell, B. and Viamontes, J. (1973). 'Effect of alcohol on short term memory in alcoholics.' *Br. J. Psychiat.* **122,** 93

Goodwin, D. and Hill, S. Y. (1973). 'Short term memory and the alcohol blackout.' *Ann. N. Y. Acad. Sci.* **215,** 195

Gross, M. M., Goodenough, D. R., Hastey, J. M. Rosenblatt, S. M. and Lewis, E. (1972). 'Sleep disturbances in alcoholic intoxication and withdrawal.' In *Recent advances in the study of alcoholism.* Ed. by N. K. Mello and J. H. Mendelson. Washington, D. C. U. S. Govt. Printing Office

Gross, M., Lewis, E. and Nagarajan, M. (1973). 'An improved quantitative system for assessing the acute alcoholic psychoses and related states (T. S. A. and S. S. A.).' In *Alcoholic intoxication and Withdrawal,* Ed. by M. M. Gross, New York; Plenum Press

Harfast, M. J., Greene, J. G. and Lasalle, F. G. (1967). 'Controlled trial comparing amobarbital and chlormethiazole in alcohol withdrawal syndrome.' *Q. Jl Stud. Alcohol* **28,** 641

Hore, B. D. (1972). 'Psychiatric emergencies.' *Br. J. Hosp. Med.* **8,** 285

Isbell, M., Fraser, H. F., Wikler, A. Belleville, R. D. and Eisenman, A. J. (1955). 'An experimental study of the etiology of "rum fits" and delirium tremens.' *Q. Jl Stud. Alcohol* **16,** 1

Jonnson, C., Cronholm, B. and Izikowitz, S. (1962). 'Intellectual changes in alcoholics—psychometric studies on mental sequelae of prolonged intensive abuse of alcohol.' *Q. Jl Stud. Alcohol* **23,** 221

Kaim, S. C., Klett, C. J. and Rothfield, B. (1971). 'Treatment of the acute alcohol withdrawal state—a comparison of four drugs.' In *Treatment of the alcohol withdrawal syndrome.* Ed. by F. A. Seixas. New York; National Council on Alcoholism

Kessel, N. and Grossman, G. (1961). 'Suicide in alcoholics.' *Br. Med. J.* **2,** 1671

Knott, D. G. and Beard, J. D. (1971). 'Diagnosis and therapy of acute withdrawal from alcohol.' In *Treatment of the alcohol withdrawal syndrome.* Ed. by F. A. Seixas, New York; National Council on Alcoholism

Mendellson, J. H. (1964). *Q. Jl Stud. Alcohol* Supplement No. 2, p. 9

Mendellson, J. H., Ogata, M. and Mello, N. K. (1969). 'Effects of alcohol ingestion and withdrawal on magnesium states of alcoholics - clinical and experimental findings.' *Ann. N. Y. Acad. Sci.* **162,** 934

Robins, E., Murphy, G. E., Wilkinson, R. H., Gassner, S. and Kaye, S. J. (1959). 'Some clinical considerations in the prevention of suicide based on a study of 134 successful suicides.' *Am. J. publ. Hlth* **49,** 888

Ryback, R. S. (1971). 'The continuum and specificity of the effects of alcohol on memory.' *Q. Jl Stud. Alcohol* **32,** 995

Seixas, F. A. (Ed.) (1971). *Treatment of the alcohol withdrawal syndrome.* New York; National Council on Alcoholism

Sereny, G. and Kalant, H. (1965). 'Comparative evaluation of chlordiazepoxide and promazine in treatment of the alcohol withdrawal syndrome.' *Br. med. J.* **1,** 92

Shepherd, M. (1961). 'Morbid jealousy: some clinical and social aspects of a psychiatric syndrome.' *J. ment. sci.* **107,** 687

Skillicorn, S. (1955). 'Presenile cerebellar ataxia in chronic alcoholics.' *Neurology, Minneap.* **5,** 627

Stein, L. I., Wiles, D. and Ludwig, A. M. (1968). 'Loss of control phenomena in alcoholics.' *Q. J. Stud. Alcohol* **29,** 598

Tavel, M. E., Davidson, and Batterton, T. D. (1961). 'A critical analysis of mortality associated with delirium tremens.' *Am. J. med. Sci.* **18,** 242

Tumarkin, B., Malls, L. and Baker, C. P. (1955). 'Cerebral atrophy due to alcoholism in young addicts.' *U. S. arm. Forces med. J.* **6,** 67

Victor, M. (1962). 'Alcoholism.' In *Baker's Textbook of neurology*. Vol. 2, chap. 22. New York; Harper & Row

Victor, M., (1970). 'The alcohol withdrawal symptoms—theory and practice.' *Postgrad. Med.* **47,** 68

Victor, M. (1971). 'Treatment of alcoholic intoxication and the withdrawal syndrome.' In *Treatment of the alcohol withdrawal syndrome*. Ed. by F. A. Seixas. New York; National Council on Alcoholism

Victor, M. and Hope, J. M. (1958). 'The phenomenon of auditory hallucinations in chronic alcoholism.' *J. nerv. ment. Dis.* **126,** 451

Victor, M., Herman, K. and White, E. E. (1957). 'A psychological study of the Wernicke—Korsakoff syndrome.' *Q. Jl Stud. Alcohol* **20,** 467

Wolfe, S. M. and Victor, M. (1969). 'The relationship of hypo-magnesaemia and alkalosis to alcohol withdrawal symptoms.' *Ann. N. Y. Acad. Sci.* **162,** 973

11

ALCOHOL INGESTION, ALCOHOLISM AND CRIMINAL BEHAVIOUR

This chapter is concerned with two principal areas; firstly, the association between drinking alcohol and subsequent criminal behaviour, and secondly, the contribution alcoholics make to criminal populations.

DRINKING ALCOHOL AND SUBSEQUENT CRIMINAL BEHAVIOUR

Alcohol ingestion in both criminal and victim has been claimed to be a factor in criminal acts. This has been applied particularly to acts of violence and sex. However, unless such ingestion is to be considered an epiphenomenon of no great importance, it has to be shown very clearly that alcohol ingestion was directly associated with the subsequent crime in a causative sense. Two different methods have been used to link drinking alcohol and criminal behaviour. The first, which is of a broad general nature, looks at overall drinking patterns in a community and levels of offences. Thus McGeorge (1962—63) in Australia records that following a reduction in hotel drinking after the First World War, there was a fall in crimes of violence and sex offences as well as a fall in attempted suicide in that country. In Britain the Office of Health Economics has emphasized how reduced drinking after the legislation of the First World War was followed by a reduction in public drunkenness offences. In the U. S. A. it has been shown that at week-ends there are increases in both serious crimes and drinking (Wolfgang and Strohm, 1956). Clearly, these types of studies, whilst of interest, can do no more than suggest some general association between drinking alcohol and subsequent crimes.

The second method has been to attempt, in individual criminal acts, to make a link. The best way would be to obtain objective evidence of alcohol ingestion prior to the crime. Such evidence would be of most value if it were chemical, that is, levels in blood or urine measured very soon after the crime was committed. Such measurements should be accompanied by observations as to the effect the alcohol had, such as measures of intoxication. It has to be admitted that such 'hard evidence' is rarely forthcoming. Thus Wolfgang and Strohm (1956), examining criminal homicides' records over a period of five years in Philadelphia, were able to record only previous absence of drinking in the offender or victim as rated by the police at the time of the offence. In 44 per cent of cases, alcohol ingestion was considered to have taken place in both victim and offender, in 11 per cent in the offender only, and in 9 per cent in the victim only. The authors emphasize that such entries 'should not be construed as causal'. McGeorge (1962–63), in New South Wales, records for a series of 60 criminals jailed for murder or attempted murder that 21 per cent had been 'drinking to excess' at the time of the offence. This term is not, however, defined. Wolfgang and Strohm (1956) quote an important study by Shupe, who analysed blood and urine for alcohol content in 882 offenders arrested during or immediately after a felony. Looking at cases of murder or manslaughter in relation to other types of offences, he considered that the chances were still better than 4 to 1 that these types of offences were committed by persons under the influence of alcohol. Other techniques have been used to examine the relationship using autopsy material. Results have varied; thus Spain, Bradess and Eggston (1951), whilst finding that 27 per cent of violent-death victims had alcohol present in brain or liver at death concluded that it was not usually in amounts that would endue intoxication. Conversely, Le Roux and Smith (1964) found that 50 per cent of homicide victims had tissue alcohol levels > 150 mg %.

Apart from crimes of violence the other principal area where the link has been examined is sexual crimes. Thus McGeorge records alcohol involvement in 9 out of 16 cases of rape and in 26 per cent of indecent assaults on adult females. He also states that as regards indecent assaults on adult males 75 per cent were intoxicated at the time of arrest and that 13 out of 28 cases of indecent exposure were 'under the influence' when arrested. Amir (1967), examining records of the Philadelphia Police Department on rape offences, finds alcohol present in victim and subject in 21.1 per cent, in victim only in 9.6 per cent, and in offender only in 2.9 per cent. The method was, in effect, identical with that of 'Wolfgang and Strohm'. Amir also examines results in other studies and shows how widely they vary. He considers one reason may be that they are dealing with different samples; for example, studies claiming high levels in offender populations may have been people easily apprehended because they were drunk. He states,

'The analysis of the literature indicates disagreement and inconsistency as to the role of alcohol in the crime of rape.' It is clear that, despite the general assumption linking drinking alcohol and subsequent criminal acts, much further work is required on differing samples of offenders using chemical tests of alcohol levels and careful assessment of degree of intoxication.

The question of how far criminal responsibility is regarded by the courts as being affected by intoxication is a very complex one and beyond the scope of this book. Important review are those of East (1948), Scott (1949), Thompson (1956) and Whitlock (1963) and in relation to the U. S. A. the article by Moore (1966) is recommended.

CONTRIBUTION OF ALCOHOLISM TO CRIMINAL POPULATIONS

It is important here to be clear as to what constitutes alcoholism and what constitutes crime, and more particularly what type of offenders are being discussed. Studies linking the two have come from many countries and some of these are described below. In Australia, McGeorge (1962–63), using police statistics over a three year period in New South Wales claims that 26 per cent of murderers, 54 per cent of these committing assault and robbery, 49 per cent of those breaking in and stealing, and 25 per cent of sex offenders against the female were alcohol addicts, 'alcohol addicts' being defined as applying to the 'heavy drinker' in the Alcoholics Anonymous classification. Robinson, Patten and Kew (1965) in Belfast considered that 55.6 per cent of successive offenders admitted to prison during a period in 1963 gave a history of alcoholism, although this was not defined. Only 54 out of the population of 566 had ever received treatment for the condition. This is reminiscent of data presented in Chapter 7 ('Prevalence') which showed how few people labelled as alcoholics in community surveys had received treatment. Gibbens and Silberman (1970) examined 404 prisoners and ex-prisoners from three contrasting London prisons, and excluded all those serving sentences of less than 28 days (which includes nearly all those sentenced for drunkenness itself). Eighteen per cent of the sample population admitted to a history of excessive drinking to the extent that it interfered seriously with their social adjustment.

In relation to female prisoners, Woodside (1961) has commented on the characteristics of females with drinking problems admitted to a London prison during one month in 1960. The majority were middle-aged, and had a history of unskilled work records, and they came from the two lowest social levels (classes IV and V). Some had an astronomical number of convictions. Thus three women had 131, 124 and 108 convictions respectively.

An important paper from the U.S.A. is that of Guze *et al.* (1962). They carried out psychiatric assessments on 223 male offenders including those due for release and those on parole and probation. Alcoholism was very carefully defined. For a diagnosis to be made, symptoms had to be present in at least two of the following five groups. *Group 1* included (a) tremors or any other manifestations of delirium tremens or a history of cirrhosis, (b) impotence associated with drinking, (c) alcoholic blackouts, (d) alcoholic 'binges' or 'benders'; *Group 2* included (a) drinking every day, (b) drinking the equivalent in terms of alcohol content of over 54 oz (1500 g) whisky, (c) being unable to answer questions concerning frequency or quantity, this being interpreted as evasiveness; *Group 3* included (a) subject had not been able to stop when he wanted to, (b) subject tried to control drinking by allowing himself to drink only in certain circumstances such as only after 5 p.m. or only at weekends, and only with other people, (c) drinking before breakfast, (d) drinking non-beverage forms of alcohol; *Group 4* included (a) arrests for drinking, (b) traffic difficulties associated with drinking, (c) trouble at work because of drinking, (d) fighting associated with drinking; *Group 5* included (a) subject felt he drank too much, (b) family objected to his drinking, (c) other people objected to his drinking, (d) he lost friends because of his drinking, (e) he felt guilty about drinking. Using these criteria, 96 (43 per cent) were felt to be suffering from alcoholism. The alcoholic group (mean age 24 years) were more likely to have a family history of alcoholism, more likely to have attempted suicide, typically had spent more time wandering around the country, and experienced more arrests and job difficulties and had been more involved in fights.

Edwards, Hensman and Peto (1971) have published an important critical review on the whole subject and describe various methodological problems in this field, including (a) lack of definition of drinking problem, alcoholic, etc., (b) the nature of the prison sample is not always clearly shown, and (c) lack of independent validation of drinking behaviour. It should be added that this last criticism could be applied to many studies of drinking behaviour apart from those relating to criminal populations. Edwards and co-workers examined two subgroups of prisoners. There were 88 consecutive male prison admissions over a six month period, and 312 men serving sentences of a year or more. Alcohol dependence was defined and graded. In relation to severe dependence, 11 per cent of the long-term prisoners fell into this category, serving sentences for drunkenness, and 19 per cent were similar prisoners serving non-drunkenness offences. If heavy drinking alone (defined as 10 pints (5.7 litres) of beer per day or more) was used as a context, 73 per cent of the short-term drunkenness offenders satisfied it, as did 14 per cent of the long-term.

Whilst different prison samples will give different percentages of alcoholics, studies such as those of Edwards and co-workers support the general view that at least for male offenders alcohol-dependent subjects make an important contribution to prison populations which in Britain are already over-congested. Hence the interest in this and other countries to deal with such people at a much earlier stage before they become either persistent drunken offenders or long-serving criminals. Eastern European and American centres have pioneered attempts to 'decriminalize the drunken offender', that is, to offer the drunken offender, and hence potential alcoholic, early detection and rehabilitation.

The Eastern European facilities seem to vary from sobering-up stations with minimal rehabilitative facilities to more extensive systems of care resembling those described by workers in St. Louis, Missouri (Pittman and Gordon, 1958). The whole question of the 'Drunkenness offence' was reviewed at a symposium in London in 1969 (see Cook, Gath and Hensman, 1969).

In Britain at the time of writing, three experimental centres are being planned following the Home Office report on the 'drunken offender' (Home Office, 1971), so the subject will shortly become of practical concern here. It would appear likely that the police will have the option of taking a drunken offender to such a centre, but this act and remaining in the centre is likely to be voluntary. Following detoxification and assessment, suitable subjects will then be offered immediate help with rehabilitation using a range of facilities such as specialized hospital in-patient and out-patient units, Alcoholics Anonymous, and community facilities such as 'half-way houses'. In relation to rehabilitation of those already in prison, certain general points should be mentioned. Firstly, the population of alcoholics is mixed; it will contain youthful offenders relatively early in their drinking careers, as well as older chronic offenders who may well have grave difficulties coping with non-institutional life apart from the alcoholism. Secondly, in Britain at any rate, there is rarely any systematic link between prison and alcoholism rehabilitation programmes in society. Even if such a link exists, Myerson *et al.* (1961) have shown the considerable difficulties which occur. They carried out an experiment in which *prior* to discharge, an attempt was made by social workers to build a relationship with offenders (in this case female) and to provide an immediate link to an alcoholism treatment programme (out-patient and emergency ward admission). On leaving prison only 18 out of the 49 'continued the therapeutic relationship or used the facilities of the hospital to a therapeutic advantage' and 20 never appeared at the clinic after discharge from the prison. It may well be that hospital-based facilities are not suitable treatment vehicles for such offenders. Rubington (1966) has explained how the social role of chronic drunken offenders is more often the result of networks of social relations rather than the product of any individual attributes, and he views the behaviour as a consequence of 'Skid Row' social norms. He suggests that the 'half-way house' is a more appropriate method of rehabilitation. The work of Cook, Morgan and Pollak (1968) in this field in Britain is described later (Chapter 14). Such hostels are, however, rare in this country, and considerably more requires to be done in developing such facilities and linking them with prison medical and social services.

REFERENCES

Amir, M. (1967). 'Alcohol and forcible rape.' *Br. J. Addict.* **62,** 219

Cook, T., Gath, D. and Hensman, C. (1969). *The drunkenness offence.* Oxford; Pergamon Press

Cook, T., Morgan, H. G. and Pollak B. (1968). 'The Rathcoole experiment.' *Br. Med. J.* **1,** 240

East, W. N. (1948). 'Medico-legal aspects of alcoholism.' *Br. J. Addict.* **45,** 93

Edwards, G., Hensman, C. and Peto, J. (1971). 'Drinking problems amongst recidivist prisoners.' *Psychol. Med.* **5,** 388

Gibbens, T. and Silberman, M. (1970). 'Alcoholism amongst prisoners.' *Psychol. Med.* **1,** 73

Guze, S. B., Tuason, V. B., Catfield, P. B., Stewart, M. A. and Picken, B. (1962). 'Psychiatric illness and crime with particular reference to alcoholism—a study of 233 criminals.' *J. nerv. ment. Dis.* **134,** 512

Home Office (1971). Report on the 'habitual drunken offender.' London; H. M. S. O.

Le Roux, L. C. and Smith, L. S. (1964). 'Violent deaths and alcoholic intoxication.' *J. forens. Med.* **11,** 131

McGeorge, J. (1962–63). 'Alcohol and crime.' *Medicine Sci. Law* **3,** 27

Moore, R. A. (1966). 'Legal responsibility and chronic alcoholism.' *Am. J. Psychiat.* **122,** 748

Myerson, D. J., Mackay, J. Wellens, A. and Neiberg, N. (1961). 'A report of a rehabilitation programme for "alcoholic woman prisoners".' *Q. Jl Stud. Alcohol* Suppl. 1, p. 151

Pittman, D. and Gadon, C. W. (1958). *'Revolving Door': a study of the chronic police court inebriate.* Glencoe, Illinois; The Free Press

Robinson, C. B., Patten, J. W. and Kew, W. S. (1965). 'A psychiatric assessment of criminal offenders.' *Medicine Sci. Law* **5,** 140

Rubington, E. (1966). 'The chronic drunkenness offender.' *Ann. Am. Acad. political soc. Sci.* **315,** 65

Scott, E. M. (1949). 'Alcoholism in criminal behaviour.' In *Mental abnormality and crime*. Ed. by L. Radzinowicz and J. W. C. Turner, London: Macmillan

Spain, D. M., Bradess, V. A. and Eggston A. A. (1951). 'Alcohol and violent death.' *J. Am. med. Ass.* **146,** 334

Thompson, G. N. (1956). 'Legal aspects of pathological intoxification.' *J. soc. Ther.* **2,** 182

Whitlock, F. A. (1963). *Criminal responsibility and mental illness*. London; Butterworths

Wolfgang, M. E. and Strohm, R. B. (1956). 'The relationship between alcohol and criminal homicide.' *Q. Jl Stud. Alcohol* **17,** 411

Woodside, M. (1961). 'Women drinkers admitted to Holloway Prison during February, 1960.' *Br. J. Criminol.* **1,** 221

12

DRINKING PROBLEMS AND MARRIAGE

A major complication of alcohol dependence is its effect on the marital situation. Bacon (1945) in Connecticut showed that compared to the normal age-comparable male population, and to two groups of offenders (traffic violations and those arrested for breach of the peace), arrested inebriates were more likely to have never married and if married were more likely to be separated from their spouse. The failure to marry appeared to arise prior to excessive drinking as they failed to marry at the expected time and factors believed responsible for this included their increased mobility, low socio-economic status, inability to maintain productive employment and their degree of social isolation. In relation to the degree of separation the sample was described as belonging to the lower social class. Its members had poor work records, were unlikely to be in professional occupations and were lower-paid. This type of socially-disintegrated individual is, of course, only *one* sample of those with drinking problems. Bailey (1961), in her most important review paper, stresses how this stereotype became accepted for all those with such problems until studies in the 1950s appeared, particularly that of Strauss and Bacon (1951). These males were found to have married to the same extent at ages comparable to the normal population but 26 per cent were divorced or separated. Kephart (1954), in examining divorce petitions in Philadelphia, found that excessive drinking was the third most frequent case of complaint when the wife was the plaintiff and indeed was more frequent than cruelty and adultery. In relation to social class, apart from the lowest group of social class, he found that further down the scale there occurred the greatest percentage of cases in which drinking was a cause of complaint. This relative tolerance of the middle classes would find support from the study in the Shadel Sanatorium (a private hospital for alcoholics)

(Wellman, Maxwell and O'Hollaren, 1957), where 75 per cent of clients were still living with their wives. Bailey, in her study of outcome of alcoholic marriages, also found that in the group where divorce had occurred there were greater degrees of deviance, more court appearances, limited education and lower status. In Kephart's study, just over a quarter of cases with wife as plaintiff cited excessive drinking (only 4 per cent where male was plaintiff). Further, in the cases of desertion by the male he examined, he found approximately one quarter were associated with excessive drinking. In the study in general practice already described (Hore and Wilkins, 1976), 53 per cent of the sample of alcoholics seen in the practices were experiencing serious marital problems, which were the commonest single social problem.

Drinking behaviour liable to cause social difficulties would appear to be associated with marital break-up, to a high degree of frequency. Over the past twenty-five years there have been many descriptions of the wives of alcoholics, and a dichotomy has developed between those (usually with psychoanalytical training) who see the wife to have characteristic personality patterns which have contributed in a major way to their spouse's drinking problem and those who see the wife's behaviour as a reaction to living with a drinking problem. It is important to note, however, that these studies both see the alcoholic marriage in isolation and pay scant regard to important data on other crisis (non-alcoholic) marital situations. Orford (1974), in a most important review, emphasizes this point. He states, 'Marriages selected because of the presence of alcoholism or problem drinking are still studied and discussed as if the problems experienced within them and the abnormalities displayed by them are unique, and there is virtually no recognition of the possibility that these problems and abnormalities might be more general.'

Amongst authors who see characteristic personality patterns are Futterman, Lewis and Whalen. Futterman (1953) admits that his descriptions represent a certain oversimplification. Wives are said to 'nag' and take up a controlling efficient role, often with a motherly protective attitude to their husband with a desire to emphasize his inadequacies. Lewis (1954) has emphasized how wives of alcoholics rarely take any blame for the situation on themselves, and consistently use projection and displacement. He considered that such women show certain personality characteristics, notably 'dependency difficulties and sexual immaturity'. He affirms that a certain number (unspecified) had experienced emotional deprivation in childhood. Whalen (1953) has described evocatively four types of women married to alcoholics, these descriptions being based on cases seen in a Family Service Agency. The types are (a) 'Suffering Susan', who is considered to be basically masochistic but overtly an excellent manager, meek and conventional; (b) 'Controlling Catherine', a dominating personality whose main role seems to have always been a desire and a belief that she can sort him out; (c) 'Wavering Winifred'—this type is commoner than the previous two example. Here ambivalence is marked; she is a basically insecure personality who hatches out lame ducks and is felt to enjoy the fuss and sympathy given to her in this situation; (d) 'Punitive Polly', an aggressive dominating female primarily interested in her career who relates only to vulnerable men.

These and other authors emphasize how such women may marry more than one person with a drinking problem and how cessation of the husband's drinking may be associated with psychological breakdown on their part. All these studies are primarily case descriptions and lack controls and in addition it is difficult to be certain whether these characteristics precede or follow upon the husband's drinking. They have been severely criticized by Jackson (1954). She states, 'The studies of wives of alcoholics impute psychological traits to the wife as judged from her behaviour *after* her husband has reached an advanced stage of alcoholism and posit that these psychological traits would have been found *prior* to the onset of drinking. None of the articles conceptualize the behaviour of the wife or the personality traits inferred from this behaviour as a reaction to a cumulative crises in which the wife experiences progressively more stress.' Bailey (1961) has commented, 'Studies to date have also been largely characterized by selective samples, and lack of controls.' Though each author cited has cautioned about overgeneralization, nevertheless the reader tends to emerge with an impression from the psychiatric and social case work that the 'classic' description of the dominant controlling wife and the weak dependent husband applies universally.

Jackson (1954) has seen the wives' behaviour in terms of her reaction to the family crises engendered by the husband's drinking. Her account is based on Alcoholics Anonymous (A. A.) members over a period of several years' observation of groups and discussion with clients. In effect she considers (although the time sequence will vary from case to case) that a common pattern emerges. Firstly, there is denial on the wife's part (this has already been described in Chapter 2), then attempts to cover up and hide, with increasing social isolation; this is followed by an attempt to take over control, with increasing independence and eventual separation. If reunion occurs with the husband sober, considerable reorganization will have to occur with the wife allowing the husband to 'take over the reins again'. The latter role change may be very difficult for the wife, who may also have to cope with her husband's involvement in A. A. and other organizations.

Whether such clear-cut stages are regularly seen and whether such a pattern is unique to alcoholic marriages would seem doubtful. Orford (1974) makes both these points and in relation to the latter describes how similar patterns are seen in other situations such as war, unemployment, mental illness in the spouse and also in couples undergoing marital counselling for non-alcoholic problems.

Further, the familiar statements regarding role transfer assume male domination to have been the norm. However, Orford (personal communication, 1974) found in a study of alcoholic marriages that 23 per cent had wife dominance in the first year. Further, in over half the couples the husband's drinking problem predated the marriage, making it extremely difficult to assess what the marital role had been before the onset of the drinking problem.

Bailey (1961) has stated that in addition to overgeneralization, highly-selected samples, and a paucity of quantitative data, a further serious difficulty has arisen from these two approaches. She states, 'Research on alcoholism and the family has suffered from several serious defects not the least of which has been failure to achieve an integrated psycho-social approach. The psychiatric focus on neurotic interaction and the sociological approach through stress theory have preceded with a minimum of cross fertilization.' One should add, as stated above (Orford, 1974) that these studes have also occurred in isolation from studies of marriage in other case situations.

INTERPERSON PERCEPTION AND MARRIAGE

Recent studies have emphasized the manner in which partners in an alcoholic marriage perceive themselves and their partner. Thus Kogan and Jackson (1963), in a controlled study, found that wives described their husbands as 'sceptical, distrustful and possessing few socially-desirable characteristics' and as 'failing to fulfil the expressive marital role'. Perhaps more important are studies where discrepancy is measured between spouses' view of their alcoholic partner and that of the alcoholic partners' view of themselves. Drewery and Rae (1969) found a significantly larger discrepancy in interperson perception between alcoholic males and their wives compared with a control group. This difference was not attributable to greater understanding within this group but due to the operation of a stronger masculine stereotype response set in this group. Particularly larger discrepancies in the alcoholic marriage group were of couples scoring high on the psychopathic score of the Minnesota Multiphasic Personality Inventory.

As Orford (1974) emphasizes, congruence between husbands and wives in non-alcoholic studies in relation to such characteristics as male assertiveness appear to be important, differentiating happy from non-happy marriages. Non-alcoholic marriages lacking this congruence may be as unhappy as alcoholic marriages.

MANAGEMENT OF THE ALCOHOLIC SPOUSE

Attempts at group work and case work have been described. Most authors who are describing small numbers of cases emphasize the difficulty and lack of success of their efforts.

Attempts at group work have been made by Gliedman *et al.* (1956) and McDonald (1956). The former describe concurrent group sessions of both alcoholics' wives and male alcoholics. Difficulty was experienced in both groups in terms of attendance and indeed in taking up treatment. The wives appeared the more powerful and effective. Even when there was improvement in the husband's drinking there appeared little improvement in the relationship. McDonald describes patterns of behaviour in wives' groups. These included attempts to monopolize the therapist, high anxiety levels in the unstructured situation, marked heterogeneity of behaviour, unreliable attendance, and the group generally lacked cohesiveness.

Despite these discouraging statements the alcoholic spouse does need support and encouragement as she is frequently isolated. Attendance at Alanon (the sister organization of A. A. for relatives of alcoholics) or similar group should be encouraged.

Studies have shown that the personality of the wife and the 'cohesiveness' of marriages are prognostic variables in treatment outcome. Thus Rae (1972) found that a wife's high psychopathic deviance score on the M. M. P. I. was associated with a poor prognosis. Orford (personal communication, 1974) found that the more cohesive a marriage was 'at intake' the better was the outcome of the husband's drinking at follow-up.

'Cohesiveness' was characterized by husband's and wife's reports of relatively high levels of affection, statements indicating that husbands were relatively involved in family tasks, optimism *re* the future of the marriage and favourable description by wife or husband when he was sober. An early study is that of Price (1945). Of 20 wives of alcoholics none had insight into their husband's personality difficulties and all blamed the situation on factors outside their husbands or the marriage. Ten particularly did not want help. Lewis (1954) has emphasized the

ambivalence existing in such wives and that most wives wish for controlled drinking rather than abstinence. There seemed to be four main
factors which made them seek help. These were economic, resentment
by adolescent children and others of drinking behaviour, strain on the
woman's health and fear of loss of husband. Their behaviour was
characterized by 'wavering' that is, repeated threats of separation which
never materialized except in terms of sexual deprivation. He emphasizes
that the case worker must expect strong defences, and make the spouse
understand she sees her need for them. Further, casework must be
wider than the 'alcohol problem', examining difficulties in the wife and
marriage. Baldwin (1947) has also stressed the difficulty in family
casework where one family member is an alcoholic. An assessment was
made of outcome of such family casework. In 24 unselected cases only
one quarter were slightly improved and half showed no improvement.
Nine never attended more than once. In these 24 cases and a further 5
there were no obvious factors for differentiating cases with good or bad
outcome. All that could be said of the good-outcome cases was that
'there seemed to be a meeting between clients who were most able to
be helped and case workers who could help them'.

REFERENCES

Bacon, S. O. (1945). *Inebriety, social integration and marriage* (Memoirs of the
    Section on Alcohol Studies, Yale University, No. 2). New Haven, Connecticut;
    Hillhouse Press
Bailey, M. B. (1961). 'Alcoholism and marriage—a review of research and profes-
    sional literature.' *Q. Jl Stud. Alcohol* 22, 81
Baldwin, D. S. (1947). 'Effectiveness of casework in marital discord with alco-
    holism.' *Smith Coll. Stud. soc. Work* 18, 69 No. 2
Drewery, J. and Rae, J. B. (1969). 'A group comparison of alcoholic and non-
    alcoholic marriages using the interpersonal perception technique.' *Br. J.
    Psychiat.* 115, 287
Futterman, S. (1953). 'Personality trends in wives of alcoholics.' *Br. J. psychiat.
    soc. Wk* 23, 27
Gliedman, L. H., Rosenthal, D., Frank, J. D. and Nash, H. T. (1956). 'Group
    therapy of alcoholics with concurrent group meetings of their wives.' *Q. Jl
    Stud. Alcohol* 17, 655
Hore, B. D. and Wilkins, R. H. W. (1976). 'A general practitioner's study of the
    commonest presenting symptoms of alcoholism.' *J. R. Coll. gen. Practnrs*
    26, 140
Jackson, J. K. (1954). 'The adjustment of the family to the causes of alcoholism.'
    Q. Jl Stud. Alcohol 15, 562
Kephart, W. M. (1954). 'Drinking and marital disruption—a research note.' *Q. Jl
    Stud. Alcohol* 15, 63
Kogan, K. L. and Jackson, J. K. (1963). 'Some role perceptions of wives of
    alcoholics.' *Psychol. Rep.* 9, 119

Lewis, M. E. (1954). 'The initial contact with wives of alcoholics.' *Soc. Casework* **35,** 8

McDonald, D. E. (1956). 'Mental disorders in wives of alcoholics.' *Q. Jl Stud. Alcohol* **19,** 125

Orford, J. (1974). 'Alcoholism and marriage, the argument against specialism.' *Jl Stud. Alcohol* **36,** 1537

Price, G. M. (1945). 'A study of wives of twenty alcoholics.' *Q. Jl Stud. Alcohol* **5,** 620

Rae, J. B. (1972). 'The influence of the wives on the treatment outcome of male alcoholics—a follow up study of two years.' *Br. J. Psychiat.* **120,** 601

Strauss, R. and Bacon, S. D. (1951). 'Alcoholism and social stabilty. A study of occupational integration in 2023 male clinic pateitns.' *Q. Jl Stud. Alcohol* **12,** 231

Wellman, W. M., Maxwell, M. A. and O'Hollaren, P. (1957). 'Private hospital alcoholic patients and the conception of the typical alcoholic.' *Q. Jl Stud. Alcohol* **18,** 388

Whalen, T. (1953). 'Wives of alcoholics—four types observed in a family service agency.' *Q. Jl Stud. Alcohol* **14,** 632

13

MANAGEMENT-I

The usual aim of management is to enable the alcohol-dependent subject to give up alcohol totally. It is felt, particularly when the stage of addiction including physical dependence has been reached, that a return to normal drinking is impossible. Although it has been claimed that this is not true for all patients (Davies, 1962; Kendell, 1965) and is sometimes regarded as unrealistic, this approach remains the standard approach of most alcoholism treatment units in Britain and of Alcoholics Anonymous (A. A.). Glatt (1972) has recently re-emphasized this view. Very recently, behavioural techniques using modified aversion stimuli triggered off by the subject's blood alcohol level and thus permitting a return to some form of controlled drinking has been introduced. At present this largely remains, however, a research procedure.

Gerard, Saenger and Wiley (1962) have questioned whether abstinence is a sufficient criterion. They attempted to examine 50 abstinent patients followed at periods of 2, 5 and 8 years after admission for treatment. Twenty-nine (54 per cent) were found to be tense, aggressive, anxious or psychotic, whilst 12 (24 per cent), whilst abstinent, lived a 'meagre life' in terms of involvement. Eleven patients (22 per cent) did seem content, but in 6 of these (12 per cent) the patient seemed as dependent on A. A. as they had been on alcohol. Only 5 (10 per cent) were considered to be independent successes. They did confirm, however, a consistent relationship between abstinence and better family relationships, physical health and social and occupational adjustment. It might be expected that on becoming abstinent a large number of alcoholics would remain tense and neurotic, etc. The value of abstinence perhaps lies in the corollary of their other findings, that is, a return to drinking is very likely to lead to disintegration of social, occupational and family life together with physical ill health. Pattison (1973) has also questioned the aims of treatment, and the danger of using abstinence as a single criterion. He describes a study examining aims of four treatment facilities. These were aversive-conditioning treatment in hospital (population of high education with good social stability), alcoholism out-patient clinics (dealing with less socially-stable, but still fairly well-integrated clients), alcoholism 'half-way houses' (patients with a history of inability to cope with life, i.e. 'low bottom' alcoholics) and the Police Farm Work Centre (dealing with the 'bottom' section of the alcoholic population). He emphasizes how the aims and philosophy are different. The first facility aims to treat the alcoholic with the prime aim of stopping drinking; the second is concerned with personal conflicts underlying alcohol misuse; the third facility aims at achieving social rehabilitation in people who could just 'cope with life' if they were not alcoholics. The final facility residents require 'some respite in life by living in an institution that will provide this with support and nurture that they cannot give themselves'. Clearly the expectations and aims of these facilities differ widely.

Emrick (1974) is carrying out an important series of reviews of the effectivenesss of treatment programmes. Despite the criticisms of the authors above, in a review of a large number of studies he found drinking outcome was a useful criterion as 'it can be concluded that drinking outcome was associated positively with outcome on dimension in the following clusters: affective, cognitive, work situation, interpersonal relationships in the home, physical condition, arrests and other legal problems . . .'.

The first and often extremely difficult task is to obtain the patient's acceptance that he or she has a problem at all. All too often the subject is not prepared to do this, and it is perhaps true that in the ordinary clinical picture this is the rule rather than the exception. Although this does not totally invalidate any hope of success (Lemere, O'Holloren and Maxwell, 1958), it is generally agreed that such acceptance is the beginning of recovery. The acceptance of the need for total sobriety is frequently just as difficult to obtain. Often pressure has to be brought by relatives, employers, etc, to induce the subject to seek help. Providing such pressure is firmly and consistently applied it can be of great value (Lemere, O'Holloren and Maxwell, 1958); often subjects are shielded from the consequences of their drinking, and the problem allowed to deteriorate until a point is reached where the reverse applies; that is, the patient becomes totally rejected, and this rejection may be irreversible even if sobriety is attained.

Although an attempt at total abstinence remains the cornerstone of treatment, it has to be accepted that alcoholics relapse (Hore, 1971) and that Edwards' comment (Edwards, 1967): 'in realistic terms the work of an alcoholism treatment service, unless it rejects its immediate failures, is largely the long-term care of people more or less frequently in difficulties', appears very relevant.

IDENTIFICATION OF PATIENTS

The general practitioner

'As a rule it seems doctors and alcoholics do not care a great deal for crossing each other's path.'

Glatt (1960)

The first stage in management of any disorder is case identification. In Britain under the National Health Service every subject is entitled to his own general practitioner. It is, therefore, extremely important that the general practitioner has a high likelihood of detecting cases. Published studies (Parr, 1954; Wilkins, 1972, 1974) support the view that in fact this is not so unless the general practitioner has special interest or experience in the problem (Pollak, 1971; Wilkins, 1974). Rathod (1967) found that approximately a quarter of 76 general practitioners who replied to a questionnaire considered problems with drinking to be 'moral' rather than 'medical'. Indirect studies in which general practitioners with no special interest in alcoholism have been asked how many alcoholics they know have found prevalence rates a sixth to an eight of those obtained from direct case identification studies in general practice (Parr, 1954; Pollak, 1971; Wilkins, 1974).

Although it is clear that the general practitioner is faced with special problems in dealing with patients with a drinking problem in that the patient may deny symptoms to the doctor, it is clear that increased identification is likely to occur only if the family doctor has a high diagnostic index of suspicion. Perhaps a parallel with myxoedema should be drawn, that is, it will be diagnosed only if it is consistently thought of. A further difficulty is that presenting symptoms may be social rather than in terms of medical morbidity. Table 4 shows the percentage of symptoms recorded by a sample of general practitioners who eventually referred the case to a regional alcoholic treatment unit (Hore and Wilkins, 1976).

Wilkins (1974) has advocated the use of an alcoholism 'at risk register' to increase case identification in general practice. In his monograph he describes the development of an 'at risk register' analogous to

TABLE 4

Symptoms Recorded by General Practitioners (n = 101) in a Group
of Alcoholics Later Referred to an Alcohol Unit (From Hore and Wilkins, 1976)*

Symptoms	Percentage of patients
Social difficulties	
(a) Marriage	52.5
(b) Work	35.6
(c) Offences against law	15.8
(d) Debts	17.8
(e) Aggressive behaviour	24.7
Medical morbidity	
(a) Gastritis	11.9
(b) Duodenal ulcer	3.0
(c) Peripheral neuropathy	4.0
(d) Cirrhosis	2.0
(e) Pneumonia	3.0
Psychiatric morbidity	
(a) Anxiety, depression or both	12.9
(b) Suicide attempts	4.9
Smelling of alcohol in the surgery	28.7

* Reproduced with permission of the *Journal of the Royal College of General Practitioners*

other 'at risk registers', for example paediatric. The 'at risk factors'
included (a) *diseases associated with alcoholism* (pancreatitis, cirrhosis
of the liver, peptic ulcer, gastritis, peripheral neuropathy, tuberculosis,
congestive heart failure of unknown origin, late-onset epilepsy,
malnutrition and obesity, haematemesis and melena, anxiety and
depression, attempted suicide), (b) *symptoms of alcohol addiction*, (c)
occupations known to have a significant incident of alcoholism (e.g.
publicans, licensees, commercial travellers), (d) *problems at work* (i.e.
absenteeism, frequent changes of job, repeated requests for sickness

certificates), (e) *accidents* (home, industrial and traffic), (f) *criminal offences*, (g) *family and marital problems*, (h) *patients seeking help for their alcoholism*, (i) *smelling of alcohol*, (j) *being a single male over 40 years of age*, (k) *having been married more than once*, (l) *living in a hostel for destitutes*, (m) *family history of abnormal drinking*, and (n) *being a relative of a patient at risk for alcoholism.*

Patients aged between 15 and 65 years of age who were thus so placed on the 'at risk register' were given a disguised questionnaire (asking about spare-time activities including drinking behaviour) if they attend the surgery during the study year. Using this technique a prevalence rate for alcohol addicts, and patients with drinking problems combined (both in terms of the present and past) was 11—18.2 per 1000 of the population. Such a prevalence rate is considerably more than other studies from general practice (Parr, 1954; Pollak, 1971) and resembles the W. H. O. estimate (see Chapter 7) based on the Jellinek formula of 11 per 1000.

It should be noted, however, that not all sources consider it fitting for the general practitioner to involve himself with alcoholics. Nicholas (1970), in questioning whether the general practitioner should be involved with alcoholism, wrote: 'To add the management of alcoholism to his duties is plainly absurd . . . the G. P. is not by disposition, character or activity suited to an interest in alcoholism.' Even more disturbing was a *British Medical Journal* editorial (1972) in which it was concluded, 'It is difficult to believe that as general practice is at present organized the family doctor is going to have much more time to help the drinker.' Why 'the drinker' is less deserving of the general practitioner's time, than other patients as this article appears to imply, is not stated.

In recent years, however, there has been a considerable upsurge in interest regarding: alcoholism in general practice. This has been reflected in attendance at symposia, etc., by general practitioners on this subject, an increase in articles and important research studies carried out in general practice (e. g. Wilkins, 1974).

Identification by other medical personnel

Patients may present, of course, to medical personnel other than family doctors. Studies in the U. S. A. have suggested that non-psychiatric medical personnel are likely to miss cases of alcoholism. Blane and his colleagues, as previously described (Chapter 8), suggested this may be the result of bias on the part of the physician and an incorrect stereotype of the alcoholic patient. Pearson (1962), examining patients on medical and surgical wards of an American hospital, found that of 29 patients with the diagnosis of alcoholism, only 12 had a history of problem drinking recorded in their clinical charts. In the U. S. A. the situation may be improving, however, for Ewing and Rouse (1970) in the same hospital 11 years later found that the recognition rate of patients with alcoholism had increased from 44 to 60 per cent.

Identification by non-medical personnel

These include a wide range of personnel, both those with a professional interest in alcoholism such as social workers, clergymen, etc., and others such as employers, organizations such as the Samaritans (a voluntary organization extending across the British Isles providing a network of counsellors who will help anyone who wishes to talk over a personal problem free of charge), and members of A. A. In addition, as will be described later, in recent years 'walk-in' counselling services have been established in some major British cities under the umbrella of the Councils of Alcoholism. Such centres enable anybody to obtain advice on a drinking problem free of charge given by experienced counsellors who may or may not be recovered alcoholics themselves.

It is clear that with all agencies the more knowledge people have and the more they see alcoholism as a condition deserving of help, the more are patients likely to receive help. Unfortunately the image of the alcoholic as a 'Skid Row' figure appears to remain a common sterotype whilst in fact it has been shown this represents only a small percentage of the total number of cases seen and represents the 'end state' of a progressive disorder.

The futility of arresting and administering petty fines to drunken offenders, of whom 40 per cent may be chronically dependent on alcohol, has at last been recognized in Britain (Home Office Report, 1971), and the procedures suggested in that report, consisting of admitting such offenders into detoxification units which are part of a comprehensive alcoholism rehabilitation service, is one technique which it is hoped will increase case identification. At the time of writing it would appear that a certain number of such units will open shortly in Britain.

ROLE OF THE HOSPITAL IN MANAGEMENT

It is important to be clear as to what are the reasons for hospital admission apart from those patients with physical or mental illnesses associated with the disorder. In Liverpool, for example, the Merseyside Council of Alcoholism considers that only one third of its clients require hospital treatment (Kenyon, 1974). It would appear there are three principal reasons for such treatment, Firstly, detoxification, secondly to provide a sheltered alcohol-free environment whereby a patient who is unable to stop drinking in the 'world outside' may at least temporarily break his drinking habit. Finally, admission may be required for the application of specialized techniques such as group therapy or aversion techniques, which are often available only in the hospital setting.

Apart from admission to hospital, many units treat patients using out-patient methods (Smith Moorhouse and Lynn, 1964; Edwards and Guthrie, 1966). Edwards and Guthrie in their study (1966) found results of out-patient treatment as effective as in-patient methods. It is probably advisable therefore that hospital treatment begins with the alcoholic as an out-patient, and admission is advised on one of the three criteria given above. Out-patient treatment usually involves making the patient aware of the seriousness of his problem (often difficult), dealing with the 'here and now reality problems', developing a supportive relationship and encouraging the patient to attend some form of group psychotherapy, such as A. A. or hospital out-patient group.

Type of hospital unit suitable for treatment

In the author's opinion it is preferable if hospitalization is required (though rarely practical) for detoxification to occur in a primary medical rather than psychiatric setting. It may be possible in mild cases for withdrawal to occur while the subject is an out-patient under the general practitioner's supervision. In terms of hospital admission as a means of interrupting the drinking bout and providing a rehabilitation service, the trend during the last twenty years in Britain has been the development of specialized alcoholism treatment units. Such units frequently do not themselves detoxify the patient but admit after the patient has been alcohol-free for several days. There are now in England and Wales over 20 such units which have been established on a regional basis and further units are being developed.

It has been pointed out that the results from such units are not necessarily superior to those from general psychiatric units (where alcoholics are mixed with other patients) run by a psychiatrist interested in alcoholism (e. g. Davies, Shepherd and Myers, 1956). It may well be that the similar results occur because of equal enthusiasm in treating such patients shown by the staff of an alcoholism treatment unit and the staff of such a general unit. In other types of general unit with a first-aid approach, however, Vallance (1965) has shown that results are inferior to those from active treatment centres. It should be pointed out also (as will be discussed below) that in the comparison of treatment from different centres even within the same country, conclusions are very difficult to reach as so many variables are associated with outcome including, possibly, wide variations in the samples from different centres.

Role of the alcoholism treatment unit

The treatment unit would appear to have the following functions. Firstly, it acts as an early-identifiable 'referral sink' to which cases can be referred. Secondly, it acts as a centre for the application of specialized techniques aimed at inducing attitude and behavioural change. It is assumed (although this has not been established) that attitudes to alcoholism are of major importance, Thirdly, it can act as a centre for research. The majority of units in Britain admit patients dependent on alcohol alone; a minority admit patients in addition who are dependent on other drugs. The question of 'mixed' units or purely alcoholic units remains controversial. The first treatment unit in this country began in the 1950s at Warlingham Park Hospital, Surrey under the charge of Dr. Max Glatt (Glatt, 1961). The fundamental premise behind such units was that instead of alcoholics being mixed with other categories of psychiatric patients they would mix only with other alcoholics. This would encourage group identification of a single common problem, and provide the appropriate environment for techniques such as group therapy.

In such units the structure attempts to resemble more that of the 'therapeutic community' than the traditional hierarchical medical model. The former term has become so abused in recent years that it is perhaps necessary to discuss this further. Admission to alcoholic units is usually controlled by staff, not patients, although all staff may participate in a staff group decision regarding admission. If possible a high nursing staff:patient ratio exists with the staff attempting to create a relaxed informal atmosphere with the patients. Patients are encouraged as a group to organize at least part of their own group activities. Attempts are made for individual problems in patients to be dealt with by the group of patients, at least in the first instance. Regular staff–patient discussion meetings are held. The cornerstone of treatment is the regular (usually daily) group therapy meetings led by a

TABLE 5
Characteristics of Patients Attending Alcoholic Units in
England and Wales (n = 334, 269 ♂, 65 ♀). (From Hore and Smith, 1975)*

Mean age

Males	42 ± 12.1 years
Females	40.5 ± 9.7 years

Educational background

Sample (n = 323)	31% Grammar school
	56% Secondary modern
Control data	23% Grammar school
	71% Secondary modern

Social class - Male patients (n = 164)

Social class	Patient sample, %
I	14
II	25
III	35
IV	12
V	14

Social class—Male patients. North-west England compared with census data

Social class	Patient sample, %	Census data, %
I	14.9	3.3
II	23.4	13.6
III	29.8	51.3
IV	14.8	20.3
V	16.9	11.4

Social stability rating [Strauss and Bacon (1951) scale] —Male patients (n = 264)

No. of points on scale	Patient sample, %
4	33
3	31
2	21
1	15
0	5

* Reproduced with permission of Churchill-Livingstone

staff member who attempts, however, to take on a non-directive, interpretative role. It is perhaps pertinent here to look at the type of patients who attend as in-patients in alcoholic units. Hore and Smith (1975) looked at samples of patients attending as in-patients in 15 of the 17 recognized units in England and Wales (Table 5).

It can be seen that these patients have an educational background higher than a control group, as indicated by the greater proportion of those with grammar school backgrounds, and that there is overrepresentation of the upper two social classes (professional and clerical) and lowest social class (unskilled workers). In terms of social stability ratings they are high, resembling very closely patients of Strauss and Bacon (1951).

Classical group psychotherapeutic teaching emphasizes the role of the therapist as non-directive, and attempts to carry out group interpretations rather than individual. It should be remembered that whilst such an approach is probably desirable with alcoholics, particularly in terms of relatively unsophisticated patients, a more directive approach may be necessary in which the therapist may find it necessary both to raise questions and to deal with individuals. It should also be remembered that the average period of time spent in such units (6–12 weeks) is very brief compared with periods patients with other psychiatric disorders spend in out-patient group therapy (usually years) or in specialized in-patient units dealing with neurotic or personality disorders.

Group psychotherapy in some units may involve the formal reading of a life history to other patients. Although the mechanism in which group therapy changes attitudes (if indeed it does) is incompletely understood, it is clear that certain of the same fundamental elements for attitude change are present in such groups as exist in alcoholism treatment units, and parallels can be drawn with groups of a religious and political nature (Frank, 1961). Firstly, there is the common problem (irrespective of other differences) shared by all patients, namely to give up alcohol. Secondly, there is an element of 'confession' with emotional *sequelae*. Thirdly, there is a clearly defined 'road back to health',.that is, by becoming sober. Finally, there is the intense group support.

Apart from group psychotherapy, other specialized techniques may be applicable. The best-known are the following.

Aversion techniques

Aversion treatment, which in essence temporarily impairs alcohol or drinking behaviour with a fear-inducing stimulus (for example nausea or electric shocks) goes back over 30 years. Such methods have been reviewed by Franks (1966). Voegtlin (1940) gives credit to Russian authors such as Markovinkov and Ichok who applied the principles from Pavlov's conditioning experiences to this particular treatment situation. Voegtlin (1940) claimed extremely good results using emetine and/or apormorphine as emetics. He claimed that approximately two thirds of patients became abstinent and remained so during the next four years. The level of abstinence for the six month period immediately following treatment was 97 per cent. The average length of stay was 5 days. It should be noted that the usual period of stay in an alcoholism treatment unit today is 6–12 weeks. Lemere and Voegtlin (1950), reporting from the Shadel Sanatorium in Seattle, reviewed 4096 patients (out of a total of 4468) who had been treated between May 1935 and October 1948. Of the patients treated, 44 per cent had been abstinent following their first treatment and of those who relapsed 879 received re-treatment. Thirty-nine per cent remained sober since their previous conditioning treatment. In terms of length of time since treatment, they claim 60 per cent remained abstinent for at least 1 year, 51 per cent for at least 2 years, 38 per cent for at least 5 years, and 25 per cent for at least 10 years. They considered their results superior to other treatments of a primarily psychotherapeutic type.

Apart from chemical aversion, electrical aversive techniques have been carried out (Kantarovitch, 1929; Hsu, 1965), electric shocks as a fear-inducing stimulus permit more accurate control of the stimulus with respect to onset, intensity and duration.

There are certain important comments that must be made of these studies. Firstly, it would appear that other elements of a psychotherapeutic nature exist in the treatment as the authors freely admit. Secondly, patients are selected by at least one factor, that of finance. At the time of the report (Voegtlin and Lemere, 1941–42) treatment were costs between $540 and $750 per patient. They comment, 'Over a hundred charity cases have been treated, but the results have been discouraging.' Many specialists obtain good results from a variety of treatments with such patients. It is difficult, therefore, to estimate whether in Britain with a wide variety of patients attending non-fee-paying alcoholism treatment units under the National Health Service, or this type of population, aversion treatments would offer superior results to techniques such as group therapy. What should be noted, however, as has already been mentioned, is the very brief period of in-patient treatment compared with that of patients undergoing group therapy even if patients do re-attend for reinforcing sessions.

Antabuse (disulfiram) and Abstem (citrated calcium carbimide)

These drugs produce physical symptoms in a patient in combination with alcohol. Patients taking such drugs theoretically being aware of this may stop to think before commencement of drinking, although it should be noted that alcoholic relapse (Hore, 1971) often appears impulsive. Wallerstein (1957) compared the effect of Antabuse treatment with conditioned reflex therapy, milieu therapy and group hypnotherapy; the most favourable results were in the former group. Patients who agree to take these drugs are often given a test dose, together with alcohol. Some authorities (Edwards, 1967) have, however, considered such controlled reactions as unjustifiably dangerous. Antabuse does produce side effects (including depression, confusional states, gastrointestinal and urinary symptoms, peripheral neuropathy, skin rashes and impotence) and more seriously can cause cardiac irregularities and even death. The original view that the reaction of Antabuse depends on its breaking alcohol down with accumulation of acetaldehyde is not universally accepted. One view as yet unestablished is that a quaternary ammonium compound which is toxic is formed. A recent development in Britain has been the use of Antabuse implants viable for six months (Malcolm and Madden, 1973). A further paper (Malcolm, Madden and Williams, 1974) suggests that any benefit produced can be attributed to psychological rather than pharmacological factors.

Apomorphine

Use of this drug has a long history in the treatment of alcoholism primarily as an aversive agent, in that combined with alcohol it can induce vomiting. Its use in sub-emetic doses has been described (Martensen-Larsen 1974), but an adequate clinical trial of its value remains to be undertaken.

The role of drugs

Drugs other than Abstem, Antabuse, etc., play a minimal role in management of the alcoholic apart from their use in the withdrawal period (see Chapter 10). It has to be borne constantly in mind that the alcoholic is frequently vulnerable to other drugs of dependence. It is only too easy, for example, to exchange alcohol dependence for barbiturate dependence in a patient who feels increasingly anxious after coming off alcohol. Patients frequently may feel anxious or miserable after they have come off alcohol, but this does not warrant the use of drugs in patients who are vulnerable to dependence. Other techniques—behaviour therapy, group therapy—should be considered first.

Psychological services

The clinical psychologist has an important part to play in the alcoholism treatment unit. Apart from involvement in psychiatric testing and psychotherapy, behaviour techniques may be of value in management. Aversive techniques have been described already. A minority of patients appear to have, in addition to their problem of alcohol dependence, excessive levels of either phobic or free-floating anxiety. Others may be excessively anxious in social situations or be extremely timid and non-assertive. Techniques such as systemic desensitization, implosion, assertive training, etc., may be of considerable value in such patients. The use of individual patient techniques in an alcoholic treatment unit run on group lines as a therapeutic community may create difficulties. Resentments by other patients towards a patient receiving individual ('special') techniques may arise because he is receiving additions to the 'basic fare'. Staff may also resent this as they consider it implies a failure on their part and the unit to provide enough. Such feeling may be reinforced by patients who seize on such treatments as indicating they are not really alcoholics. These feelings should be discussed between patients and staff. It is more likely to arise if it is believed that the group process is the 'only way to treat alcoholics'. Despite these difficulties, it is of considerable value to use such techniques and it should be the goal of any treatment service to encourage flexibility of treatment (Edwards, 1967).

Management of spouses

This has already been discussed in Chapter 12.

Results of treatments from hospital sources

Hill and Blane (1967) have written an outstanding review of the problems of assessing treatment outcome. They lay down the following conditions which are required before a specific treatment regime can be said to be effective:

1. Patients must be randomly assigned to control or treatment groups.
2. Criteria used to measure outcome must be theoretically and empirically relevant to the presumed effects of treatment; such criteria must be measurable by reliable methods which are applied before and after treatment.

They dismiss the idea of using patients as their own control with measurement of behaviour before and after treatment because one is unable to assume that non-treatment variables such as time play no part in outcome. Pointing out the ethical difficulties of their first criterion outlined above, they suggest two compromise solutions. The first is to compare treated patients with those not receiving treatment and generalize; secondly, one can compare minimal treatment groups with maximal. A difficulty here is that the two groups are likely to differ in terms of potentially important variables such as social class, social isolation, motivation, etc.

In discussion of criterion variables they point out the lack of agreed criteria for successful outcome. It is noteworthy that some authors use quantity and frequency of drinking behaviour, while others use crude categorizations into abstinence or infrequent drinking, drinking without social harm and drinking with severe social consequences. The objection to the use of abstinence alone as a criterion has already been described. Further, whatever criteria are used they are rarely subject to tests of reliability including inter rater reliability.

Other criticisms made by Hill and Blane are of absent or retrospective assessments of pre-treatment behaviour, poor follow-up in terms of percentage of patients contacted, and lack of data concerning treatment setting, specific type of treatment and criteria of selection procedures. In looking at published treatment studies it is doubtful if any fully satisfy their criteria. Even more fundamental problems exist. We know little of the natural history of alcoholism. Lemere (1953) examined life histories (obtained from relatives) of 500 deceased alcoholics. He considered 28 per cent drank themselves to death, 29 per cent continued to have a problem throughout their lives, 11 per cent stopped, 10 per cent regained partial or complete control and 22 per cent stopped during a fatal illness. Kendell and Staton (1966) attempted to compare treated and untreated alcoholics. However, many of the untreated groups received treatment at other centres.

Published studies in Britain from established centres (Davies, Shepherd and Myers 1956; Glatt, 1961; Walton, Ritson and Kennedy, 1966) have described outcome in the following terms. Outcome is assessed in relation to drinking behaviour and other variables and patients classified into three broad groups based on their behaviour in the six months subsequent to treatment, no assessment of pretreatment behaviour being made. These groups roughly correspond firstly to those totally abstinent (or almost totally abstinent) without social difficulties, those drinking, but without social difficulties, and finally those drinking with social difficulties. Approximately 30–40 per cent fall into the first category, 30 per cent into the second and 30 per cent into the last. Emrick (1974), in an important review of 271 studies of treatment outcome, concluded that about two thirds were improved or abstinent after psychological treatments. These results are superior to brief 'first-aid' measures (Vallance, 1965), but it is uncertain how much this relates to non-specific treatment variables such as time and enthusiasm. The above-quoted studies include both in-patients (Davies, Shepherd and Myers, 1956; Glatt, 1961) and mixed in-patients and out-patients. In one British study (Edwards and Guthrie, 1966), random allocation of matched groups was made to in-patient and out-patient treatments; this failed to show any advantage of in-patient methods. McCance and McCance (1969) in a carefully planned study found that comparing patients who had group therapy or aversion therapy with those in the same setting but with only general milieu treatment were unable to show any significant difference in the former two groups. More important in outcome were environmental and personality differences. There seemed to be little after-care in all groups so what are being compared are treatments of a fairly brief interval in an institution. Willems, Latemendia and Arroyave (1973) compared short-stay (mean 20 days) and long-stay (mean 82 days) hospital in-patient treatment of a group of male alcoholics and found no significant difference in outcome at 2 years follow-up.

Even if it is accepted that treatment results from such centres indicate a successful outcome for some clients, we learn little about individual groups of patients. Edwards (1968) has pointed out that variables in outcome may relate to factors other than the type of treatment methods. It would appear likely that outcome may relate (apart from treatment methods) to the personality of the subject, the social situation from which he comes and relates to his 'coping skills' and to how society treats him. It is clearly ridiculous to equate a middle-aged doctor with a high degree of social stability who is likely to be deprived of his livelihood if he continues drinking with a young unskilled labourer living rough who has not worked for several years and has numerous convictions. The fact that the former may improve and the latter not, may have nothing to do with the particular treatment method, but relates to variables such as social stability and motivation.

Over the last twenty years there have been a number of studies in the American and British literature which have attempted to delineate broad characteristics which are of value in assessing prognosis. It should be pointed out, however, that rarely has it been attempted to 'hold' certain characteristics whilst examining others; it is, therefore, difficult to be confident of the significance of individual characteristics. These characteristics include;

Age: Studies from Britain (Glatt, 1961; Rathod *et al.*, 1966) and South Africa (Wolffe and Holland, 1964) have suggested that patients in the younger age group, for example 20–30, fare worse than older patients.

The reasons are not clear. It has been suggested that young patients have not yet experienced sufficient suffering to motivate them away from drinking, that is, they have not reached 'rock bottom'. Further, they are less likely to be married and have social responsibilities and are possibly less sociably stable.

Sex: Glatt (1961) has recorded how female patients fare worse than males, which in his study could not be accounted for by such factors as psychopathy occurring more frequently in the female population. The vulnerability acceptance hypothesis of Jellinek (1960) considered that owing to the social pressures against female drinking, women who become alcoholic must be very abnormal personalities.

Social stability: This is frequently assessed in terms of being in one's own home, holding down a regular job, being married or in a permanent long-standing relationship (Strauss and Bacon, 1951). Wolffe and Holland (1964) in South Africa, as well as Davies, Shepherd and Myers (1956), and Goldfried (1964) and Pokorney, Miller and Cleveland from the U.S.A., have all considered this an important prediction of outcome. Again the problem relates to what this means. Are such patients more popular with hospital staff? Does society, including the law, treat them more kindly than the more sociably unstable? How much does such stability relate to personality characteristics including non-psychopathic traits? What contribution does the marriage partner make towards sobriety? Is the level of motivation towards sobriety (influenced by consequences of continued drinking) different in the different groups?

Personality: There appears to be general agreement (Glatt, 1961; Pokorney, Miller and Cleveland, 1968) that patients with psychopathic traits fare badly. This may be the reason that cases on probation under care of the courts referred to treatment centres fare badly. Once again, however, the reasons for this may be complex whilst it is likely that impulsiveness, inability to defer immediate gratification (including alcohol), and inability to form lasting emotional relationships are likely to militate against abstinence, it is also possible that attitude change (the essential aim of group psychotherapy) is less likely to occur (Heather, Edwards and Hore, 1975 see below), and that such patients are unlikely to attract as much sympathy and concern from members of the caring professions.

Attitudes and motivation: Pokorney, Miller and Cleveland (1968) and Moore and Murphy (1961) have emphasized how constructive attitudes, particularly the desire for treatment, are likely to produce a more favourable outcome. Thus Pokorney and co-workers found patients who failed to improve were more likely to think drinking useful, and that they could handle it. Moore and Murphy found that the greater the denial of the problem, the worse the prognosis. A recent current study in which a quantified technique of attitude change related to outcome will be described later. Research is clearly needed in this area, as group therapeutic techniques have as their essential goal the changing of attitudes or behaviour and it may well be that certain groups of patients are unlikely to have their attitudes changed by techniques currently in use.

Previous treatment: Davies, Shepherd and Myers (1956), Wolffe and Holland (1964) and Goldfried (1964) have all emphasized that patients who are being admitted for the first time have a better prognosis. This may, of course, indicate no more than that it is those cases which are least susceptible to treatment which require re-admission.

It is clear the interpreting the meaning behind these broad characteristics is extremely difficult. A recent approach in this direction has been the measurement of attitude change in groups of alcoholics and of examining how this change relates to these characteristics (Heather, Edwards and Hore, 1975). Heather and co-workers have examined changes in construing of the 'self' and construing of different 'drinking roles' during group therapy. During therapy, there was principally a change in construing of the former and not of the latter. There was a movement in relation to the self towards socially-approved roles; for example, the alcoholic saw himself more like a recovered alcoholic and more like a social drinker. Patients with low I.Q. and high clinical ratings of psychopathic deviance were less likely to show this general shift.

In relation to outcome, a poor outcome was seen in patients who, during therapy, either saw themselves as very close to a recovered alcoholic or normal drinker, or very close to an alcoholic who had not benefited from treatment. Heather and co-workers suggest the former may relapse because they test themselves out, and the latter because they see no hope.

Relapse: The frequency of relapse is high and despite earlier reports, in considering the six months after leaving hospital, it may occur at any point during this period (Hore, 1971). In a study of 22 patients seen for the most part at weekly intervals for six months, only 4 patients failed to relapse. Relapse appeared to be an impulsive form of behaviour and related temporarily in apparently half the cases to a preceding event in the patients's life. Contact with the therapist appeared to reduce the length of relapse rather than its frequency, a point not to be minimized, however, for it is often the extensive relapse that wreaks such havoc, particularly in social terms. Relapse, when it occurs, must not induce pessimism. Attempts must be made to encourage the patient to make contact early in the relapse period to minimize damage.

The patient refusing help: Some patients, despite all efforts, refuse help. In such instances the therapist's help may have to be confined to support of relatives, and imparting to the patient that should he require help at a later date this will be available.

REFERENCES

British Medical Journal (1972). Editorial, 'Planning the treatment of alcoholism.' *Br. Med. J.* **2**, 479

Davies, D. L. (1962). 'Normal drinking in recovered alcohol addicts.' *Q. Jl Stud. Alcohol* **23**, 94

Davies, D. L., Shepherd, M. and Myers, E. (1956). 'The two year prognosis of 50 alcohol addicts after treatment in hospital.' *Q. Jl Stud. Alcohol* **17**, 485

Edwards, G. (1966). 'Hypnosis in treatment of alcohol addiction.' *Q. Jl Stud. Alcohol* **27**, 221

Edwards, G. (1967). 'The meaning and treatment of alcohol dependence.' *Hosp. Med.* **2**, 272

Edwards, G. (1968). 'The role of therapy in meeting complex social problems.' *28th International Congress on Alcohol and Alcoholism. Washington, D. C.*

Edwards, G. and Guthrie, S. (1966). 'A comparison of in-patient and out-patient treatment of alcohol dependence.' *Lancet* **1**, 467

Emrick, C. D. (1974). 'A review of psychologically-orientated treatment of alcoholism – I. The use and interrelationships of outcome criteria and drinking behaviour following treatment.' *Q. Jl Stud. Alcohol* **35**, 523

Ewing, J. A. and Rouse, B. A. (1970). 'Identifying the hidden alcoholic.' *29th International Congress on Alcoholism and Drug Dependence, Sydney, Australia.* Lausanne; International Council on Alcohol and Addictions

Frank, J. (1961). *Persuasion and healing.* Baltimore; Johns Hopkins University Press

Franks, C. M. (1966). 'Conditioning and conditioned aversion therapies in the treatment of the alcoholic.' *Int. J. Addict.* **1**, 61

Gerard, D. L., Saenger, G. and Wiley, R. (1962). 'The abstinent alcoholic.' *Archs gen. Psychiat.* **6**, 83

Glatt, M. M. (1960). 'The key role of the family doctor in the rehabilitation of the alcoholic.' *J. Coll. gen. Practners Res. Newsl.* **3**, 292

Glatt, M. M. (1961). 'Treatment results in an English mental hospital.' *Acta psychiat. scand.* **37**, 143

Glatt, M. M. (1972). 'The hazy borderline of the loss of control.' *30th International Congress on Alcoholism and Drug Dependence, Amsterdam, 1972.* Lausanne; International Council on Alcohol and Addictions

Goldfried, M. R. (1964). 'Prediction of improvement in alcoholics.' *Q. Jl Stud. Alcohol* **30**, 129

Heather, N., Edwards, S. and Hore, B. D. (1975). 'Changes in construing during group therapy for alcoholism. *Q. Jl Stud. Alcohol* **36**, 1238

Hill, M. J. and Blane, H. T. (1967). 'Evaluation of psychotherapy with alcoholics.' *Q. Jl Stud. Alcohol* **28**, 76

Home Office (1971). 'Report on the habitual drunken offender.' London; H. M. S. O.

Hore, B. D. (1971). 'Factors in alcoholic relapse.' *Br. J. Addict.* **66**, 89

Hore, B. D. and Smith, E. (1975). 'Who goes to alcoholism treatment units.' *Br. J. Addict.* **70**, 263

Hore, B. D. and Wilkins, R. H. (1976). 'A general practice study of the commonest presenting symptoms of alcoholism.' *J. R. Coll. gen. Practnrs* **26**, 140

Hsu, J. J. (1965). 'Electroconditioning therapy of alcoholics—preliminary report.' *Q. Jl Stud. Alcohol* **26**, 449

Jellinek, E. (1960). *The disease concept of alcoholism*. New Haven, Connecticut; Hillhouse Press

Kantarovitch, N. V. (1929). 'An attempt at associative-reflex therapy in alcoholism.' *Nov. Reflexol., Ficiol. nerv. Sist.* **3**, 436. Abstract in *Psychol. Abstr.* **4**, 493 (1930)

Kendell, R. E. (1965). 'Normal drinking by some alcohol addicts.' *Q. Jl Stud. Alcohol* **26**, 247

Kendell, R. E. and Staton, M. C. (1966). 'The fate of untreated alcoholics.' *Q. Jl Stud. Alcohol* **27**, 30

Kenyon, W. (1974). 'The co-ordination and interaction of treatment and rehabilitation for alcoholism in the Merseyside region.' *Proceedings Alcoholism, Manchester, June 1974.* Lausanne; International Council on Alcohol and Addictions

Lemere, F. (1953). 'What happens to alcoholics.' *Am. J. Psychiat.* **109**, 674

Lemere, F., O'Holloren, P. and Maxwell, M. A. (1958). 'Motivation in the treatment of alcoholism.' *Q. Jl Stud. Alcohol* **19**, 428

Lemere, F. and Voegtlin, W. L. (1950). 'An evaluation of the aversion treatment of alcoholism.' *Q. Jl Stud. Alcohol* **11**, 199

Malcolm, M. T. and Madden, J. S. (1973). 'The use of disulfiram implantations in alcoholism.' *Br. J. Psychiat.* **123**. 41

Malcolm, M. T. Madden, J. S. and Williams, A. E. (1974). 'Disulfiram implantation critically evaluated.' *Br. J. Psychiat.* **125**, 485

Martensen-Larsen, O. (1974). 'Apomorphine or Disulfiram in the Treatment of the Alcoholic' *Proc. 20th Int. Inst. on the Prevention and Treatment of Alcoholism.* Manchester; International Council on Alcohol and Addiction, Lausanne, 1970

McCance, C. and McCance, P. F. (1969). 'Alcoholism in north-east Scotland: its treatment and outcome.' *Br. J. Psychiat.* **115**, 189

Moore, R. A. and Murphy T. C. (1961). 'Denial of alcoholism as an obstacle to recovery.' *Q. Jl Stud. Alcohol* **22**, 597

Nicholas (1970). Quoted by Wilkins, R. H. (1972). 'The detection of the abnormal drinker in general practice.' *M. D. Thesis*, University of Manchester (unpublished)

Parr, D. (1954). 'Alcoholism in general practice.' *Br. J. Addict.* **54**, 25

Pattison, E. M. (1973). 'Drinking outcomes of alcoholism treatment, abstinence, social, modified, controlled and normal drinking.' In *Alcoholism—a medical profile.* Ed. by N. Kessel, A. Hawker and H. Clarke, London; Bedsall & Co.

Pearson, W. S. (1962). 'The hidden alcoholic in the general hospital.' *N. Carol. med. J.* **23,** 6

Pokorney, A. D., Miller, B. A. and Cleveland, S. E. (1968). *Q. Jl Stud. Alcohol* **29,** 364

Pollak, B. (1971). 'Prevalence of alcoholism in a London practice.' *Practitioner* **206,** 531

Rathod, N. (1967). 'An enquiry into general practitioners' opinions about alcoholism.' *Br. J. Addict.* **62,** 103

Rathod, N., Gregor, E., Blows, D. and Thomas, G. H. (1966). 'A two year follow up study of alcoholic patients.' *Br. J. Psychiat.* **112,** 683

Smith Moorhouse, P. M. and Lynn, L. (1969). 'Analysis of the work of an outpatients units.' *Practitioner* **202,** 410

Strauss, R. and Bacon, S. D. (1951). 'Alcohol and social stability – a study of occupational integration in 2023 male clinic patients.' *Q. Jl Stud. Alcohol* **12,** 234

Vallance, M. (1965). 'Alcoholism – a two year follow up study of patients admitted to the psychiatric department of a general hospital.' *Br. J. Psychiat.* **111,** 348

Voegtlin, W. L. (1940). 'The treatment of alcoholism by establishing a conditioned reflex.' *Am. J. med. Sci.* **199,** 802

Voegtlin, W. L. and Lemere, F. (1941–42). 'The treatment of alcohol addiction.' *Q. Jl Stud. Alcohol* **2,** 717

Wallerstein, R. S. (1957). 'Hospital treatment of alcoholism – a comparative experiment study.' Menninger Clinic. Monographs Series I and II. London; Imago Publishing Co.

Walton, H. J., Ritson, E. B. and Kennedy, R. I. (1966). 'Response of alcoholics to clinic treatment.' *Br. med. J.* **2,** 1171

Wilkins, R. H. (1972). 'The detection of the abnormal drinker in general practice.' *M. D. Thesis,* University of Manchester (unpublished)

Wilkins, R. H. (1974). 'The hidden alcoholic in general practice.' London; Elek Science

Willems, P. J. A., Letemendia, F. J. J. and Arroyave, F. (1973). 'A two year follow-up study comparing short and long stay in-patient treatment of alcoholics.' *Br. J. Psychiat.* **122,** 637

Wolffe, S. and Holland, L. (1964). 'A questionnaire follow-up of alcoholic patients.' *Q. Jl Stud. Alcohol* **25,** 108

14

MANAGEMENT-II.
COMMUNITY SERVICES

THE THERAPEUTIC HOSTEL

'A man who comes to the house comes not as a faceless lodger, but immediately as a vitally important individual, a member of a community, someone who is honoured and respected who knows that every other member of that community offers caring and honest friendship'.

Griffith Edwards
(from the Giles House Charter)

Hospital treatment of any sort can be no more than a brief intervention in an alcoholic's life. There is frequently little difficulty in staying sober whilst in hospital; the essential problem remains that of staying sober 'in the world outside'. As an attempt to cater for this problem there has been the development of after-care hostels. They may or may not be a direct extension of hospital treatment. In some cases patients on leaving the hospital move to a hostel as a continuation of hospital care. In other examples perhaps the majority of clients enter the hostel from outside. In either case the essential function is to provide a community whereby sobriety is promoted. Hostels were pioneered in the U. S. A. by Myerson and Mayer (1956) and in Britain early developments were St. Luke's Rehabilitation Centre, the Rathcoole experiment (dealing with 'Skid Row' alcoholics) and hostels for alcoholics developed by the Helping Hand Organisation* (a voluntary charity).

Myerson and Mayer (1966) describe their experience over three years with a group of 101 destitute and alcoholic men whom they describe as men who in personal relationships cannot give anything but

* Address: 8 Strutton Ground, London, SW1

133

only take. Their 'protector', usually a women, 'is loved only so far as she tries to fulfil their insatiable demands'. The men resided in a dormitory unit of a city hospital where they lived and worked in the community for an indefinite period. It should be noted that this 'hostel' was part of a community programme involving employment agencies, church organizations, Alcoholics Anonymous and the Courts. An attempt was made to create a 'group spirit' and the majority of men were placed on Antabuse.

Whilst sobriety was relatively easily maintained in this sheltered setting, many men on returning to their familiar friends repeated their type of relationship and following the inevitable rejections began drinking again. Whilst 54 men improved considerably in terms of drinking very little, and spending virtually no time in jail during the three years (prior to their entering the programme a quarter of their time was spent in jails and the rest drinking), only 12 achieved independent lives free of the hospital. Myerson emphasizes that this experience raises the questions of goals of treatment. He states, 'Cure at the present state of knowledge is out of the question. Social improvement even if it implies dependency upon the hospital is perhaps the most that can be expected as a goal of therapy for this group.' It should be noted, however, that Myerson and Mayer were dealing primarily with clients of the 'Skid Row' type.

The St. Luke's Rehabilitation Centre (Ingram-Smith, 1967), which opened in 1961, was developed out of the interests of three agencies: a group of probation officers, the Welfare Department of a prison and a mission of the Methodist Church. It was aimed to help delinquent men 'whose offences were accompanied by alcoholic drinking patterns'. The house, situated in south London, had two rules: no alcohol to be consumed in the house and the residents were to 'behave like civilized human beings'. Selection, made by the staff, was fairly rigorous and admission was by referral only. Patients for whom the prognosis was poor include those who also had epilepsy, those suffering from any major psychiatric disorder, those below the age of 30 years (the best age for rehabilitation appears to be between 35 and 45 years of age), those having served a prison sentence of longer than 3 years and those unwilling to accept that they were alcoholics. Marriage, if still intact, was a favourable prognostic factor.

Employment was encouraged, as was matrimonial reconciliation if possible. Later a wing for female patients was added and plans are described to extend to a 'three-quarter-way house'. Ingram-Smith does not describe the effectiveness of the house in quantitative terms. This house is important, however, as it appears to be one of the first of its kind in Britain aimed specifically at rehabilitating alcoholics.

The Rathcoole experiment was begun in 1966 (Cook, Morgan and Pollak, 1968) in a house in the Clapham district of south London. The experiment was designed primarily to help vagrant alcoholics and the aim was to base the organization structure on therapeutic community lines although admittance to the house was controlled by the warden. Thirty-four men were admitted in the first year with an average age of 45 years. The men had been on 'Skid Row' for several years, half had fifty or more convictions for drunkenness, 70 per cent had received previous hospital treatment and all were regarded by the psychiatrist as suffering from some form of personality disorder. In terms of outcome the men fitted into three groups: those who walked out in less than 1 month (11 men), those who stayed 1–3 months (8 men) and 12 men who stayed at least 3 months. Although the latter were mainly sober throughout their time short recurrent relapses were common. The men showed a strong desire to rush into employment, in fact into jobs which were often thought inappropriate by the hostel staff. In general they had few social contacts and appeared afraid of normal social life. It should be noted the hostel was essentially supportive. The authors note the difficulty with this group of clients of adopting more active therapeutic measures. They comment, 'Men retreated from help when they most needed it and without adopting a more directive approach it was impossible to undertake a regular group discussion. They were unwilling to make majority decisions on hostel policy, and tended to present a facade of behaviour in a group, saying only what they thought would be acceptable to other men.' It should be noted that this hostel was dealing with the end state of alcoholism, i.e. 'Skid Row', and the fact that 12 men were prepared to stay for three months or more and achieved sobriety for most of this time is encouraging. Further details of the work and philosophy behind such a hostel can be derived from the Alcoholics Recovery Project annual reports (obtainable from 47 Addington Square, London SE5).

The Helping Hand Organisation opened its first house for recovering alcoholics in September 1964 in the Camberwell district of London. From that time until 31 December 1971, 171 men had been admitted, there being, 187 admissions in all (Helping Hand Report, 1972). Attempts have been made to reduce staff/client barriers with encouragement of clients to take on responsibilities which in a more authoritarian setting would be the staff's responsibility. Decisions regarding admission and discharge are made by the clients, and rules are kept to a minimum, there being essentially only two, namely that a client drinking must leave, and attendance at a weekly group therapy meeting is obligatory. Every effort is made to encourage each resident to feel the hostel is his home. In later years two further additions have been made; these are the opening of a short-stay assessment unit prior to admission to the house, and the development of self-contained flats as a second stage procedure into which men from the hostel can move. Since the opening of Giles House in 1964 the organization has opened other houses including its first home outside London at Middleton, Lancs.

An early discussion on this type of house has been made by Edwards, Hawker and Hensman (1966). They point out that two original ideas had to be abandoned; this was the insistence that the warden of such a hostel must be an alcoholic and that anyone could be admitted. In the first instance this led to the breakdown of the warden; and as regards the second, chaos was created; they state. 'Men looking for sobriety were likely to find nothing more than a drinking party in progress.' Selection (finally made by the residents themselves) was found to be essential. Difficult patients unlikely to be successful were psychopathic (manipulative or aggressive), drug addicts, 'con men' and promiscuous homosexuals.

In 1972 Richards House (named after the founder of the Helping Hand Organisation) was opened in the Greater Manchester Area. The basic organization of the house resembles that previously described (Edwards, Hawker and Hensman, 1966) but there are important differences. Firstly, the house is tied firmly to an alcoholism treatment unit and admission of clients (determined by residents) is only from men who have satisfactorily completed a period in that unit, and whilst in the house regular out-patient contact (formal and informal) is maintained with the unit. The house can be seen as an extension of the treatment programme of the unit. This has allowed the admission of more socially-integrated types of clients; indeed, in a minority of cases men who possess homes and families of their own have been admitted. These men have been such, however, that in the past they have not been able to stay sober in their type of environment. Regular group psychotherapy sessions have shown that whilst some clients may cope in terms of life function, for example work regularly, beneath their alcoholism often lie severe neurotic or personality disturbances which may need prolonged (years) periods of psychotherapy.

The descriptions of the different houses outlined above indicate that whilst they may have similar organizational structures they are dealing with different types of client. Indeed it has been said that there has been undue emphasis on the 'Skid Row' type of client. It is likely and indeed desirable that in successive years a wide variety of hostels will be developed dealing with clients at different stages of alcoholism run by both voluntary and statutory authorities. In March 1973 the Department of Social Services in Manchester opened its own hostel for alcoholics. What is essential is that accurate information is recorded of these differing types of clients attending different centres and how different client types relate to outcome and indeed to therapeutic measures in the hostel. It may well be that different therapeutic methods may be required in different types of hostel. It is also clear from work already carried out that undue pressure to discharge clients to the community must not be allowed to develop; some clients may need some form of hostel for prolonged periods, perhaps indefinitely. Second and indeed third tier hostels may be required.

As stated previously it is important to be clear what is the aim of such hostels. Are they for example places where such change is expected, so that the person will live an independent sober life again, or are they to be regarded as possibly permanent shelters?. Clinical experience suggests that it is not so difficult for people to remain sober in the hostel, it is staying sober outside that is the problem. Certainly for those hostels dealing with less integrated men, perhaps a realistic aim is that of a permanent shelter.

COUNCILS OF ALCOHOLISM

The first Council of Alcoholism in Britain was opened in 1963 in Liverpool. Since that time Councils have been established in other major cities, such as Birmingham and Manchester. The functions of such Councils would appear to be essentially threefold and different Councils have laid differing emphasis on these three functions. Firstly, there is the development of counselling services ('information centres'); secondly, the promotion of education *re* alcoholism amongst professional and lay members of the community, and finally the integration of existing treatment services and the development of new services to fill evident gaps.

As stated previously, both alcoholics and relatives may not be willing to approach their family doctor for advice regarding their drinking. Experience at Liverpool and other centres suggests that they will however approach sympathetic counsellors who are unknown to them previously and who offer immediate aid. Such counsellors may or may not be recovered alcoholics and may or may not be paid officials of the Council. Figures from three Councils indicate the likely response to such centres. Thus during the period 1 July 1963 to 30 June 1970 (Merseyside Council of Alcoholism, 7th Annual Report, 1970) 2806 new cases attend the centre at Liverpool. During 1969—1971 inclusive, the Coventry and Warwickshire Council of Alcoholism dealt with 383 cases (Coventry and Warwickshire Council of Alcoholism 2nd Annual Report, 1971), whilst during 1971 the Bristol Council dealt with 412 fresh cases (Bristol Council of Alcoholism, 2nd Annual Report, 1972). A recent review of the work of a Council of Alcoholism is that of Kenyon (Kenyon, 1974).

The types of clients attending such information centres have been examined by Edwards *et al*. (1967b). Using a structured questionnaire which could be administered to consecutive series of clients at centres in Glasgow, Gloucester and Liverpool they obtained data on 300 clients (164 men, 36 women). In relation to male clients 20 per cent were self-referred and 23 per cent had been referred to the centres by a doctor. This latter point is interesting in that it would seem to refute the argument that such centres will not be used as a referral agency by the medical profession, who are used to referring patients only to other medical agencies. The clients showed a fairly high degree of social stability in that 48 per cent were married and still living with their wives, 50 per cent were in full-time employment and only 19 per cent had served a jail sentence. It is of interest that 22 per cent believed their general practitioner was unaware of the problem and 74 per cent said they had attempted to fool their doctor, giving false reasons in order to obtain a medical certificate. In reply to those who claim there is little evidence of alcoholism in British industry it should be noted that 66 per cent and 67 per cent respectively of men stated they had been late for work at least once or twice per month in the previous year and had been absent on Monday mornings. In the previous year alone the average number of days lost from work was 86. Edwards *et al*. (1967b) compare this population with that of a previous survey (Edwards *et al*., 1966) dealing with the 'Skid Row' population. Clients attending information centres were far more socially stable in terms of persistence in a single occupation and having been and remaining married and closely resembled members of Alcoholics Anonymous, and indeed (Hore and Smith, 1975) patients attending National Health Service Alcoholic Units. It should be noted from this study that the type of client reached differs considerably from those attending the hostels previously described, which have tended to deal primarily with much more advanced cases of alcoholism who have reached an advanced stage of social disintegration.

Linked with the counselling function is the ability to refer clients immediately to a variety of treatment agencies including hospital and Alcoholics Anonymous. In some cities, such as Liverpool, agreement has been reached such that clients thought suitable can be admitted to a general medical ward for detoxification, a procedure unfortunately too rare in Britain.

The educational functions of Councils are designed to provide both public and professionals with a greater understanding of alcoholism. Activities are over a whole range of meetings from health education in schools to international conferences on alcoholism as organized by the Merseyside Council in 1971 and 1973. One of the most valuable of these activities is the Summer School on Alcoholism held originally under the auspices of the Camberwell Council of Alcoholism and now organized by the Alcohol Educational Centre*. This is a multidisciplinary intensive course with teaching based on the tutorial system. In recent years more advanced courses have been held for students who have attended such basic courses. Both types of course can be thoroughly recommended.

Integration

In developing overall services for a community it is essential to avoid duplication and isolation. In many areas alcoholism treatment services have developed on an *ad hoc* basis from a variety of voluntary and statutory agencies. Contact between agencies may be poor and little understanding of the work of others evident. Sometimes lack of understanding has given way to antagonism and the insistence that the contribution one agency is making is the 'only effective' method to deal with alcoholics.

Councils of Alcoholism can act as a central agency linking and co-ordinating the efforts of others in addition to providing treatment or diagnostic facilities. The Executives of such Councils usually include the active representatives of agencies dealing with the alcoholic in that community, such as doctors, social workers, probation officers, members of Alcoholics Anonymous, etc. From the meetings of such people an awareness of the different contributions they produce can be realized and if development of their individual activities can be co-ordinated duplication may be avoided. Such a body as a Council can also see existing gaps in services and stimulate local and national resources to fill these gaps.

ALCOHOLICS ANONYMOUS (A. A.)

This remarkable organization, founded in the U. S. A. in 1935 by two alcoholics (one a doctor), can claim to be the first agency to provide

*Address: Alcohol Education Centre, Maudsley Hospital, Denmark Hill, London SE5.

help for alcoholics on any large scale. The organization is now world-wide and it is claimed that over a million members have passed through the organization. The first group in Europe was in Dublin and shortly after this, groups were established in major cities such as London (1947) and Manchester (1948). A. A. works as a non-profit-making body without political or specific religious affiliation and welcomes anyone with a drinking problem. The aim is total sobriety and the philosophy held that whilst the alcoholic cannot control his drinking once he has started he can choose between abstinence and uncontrolled drinking. The 'key activity' is the A. A. (usually weekly) group meeting. Although quantitative data are unavailable concerning the effectiveness of change induced by contact with A. A., contact with individual members makes it evident that at least for some, membership of A. A. is associated with marked attitude and behavioural change. How is this produced? Whilst no definite answer can be given it would appear that the A. A. group meeting contains the essential elements for attitude change by group processes. This has already been outlined in relation to groups in alcoholic treatment units but will be discussed briefly again. Firstly, there is the group identification of people from whatever background sharing a common problem. Secondly, and probably more marked, there is the refusal by the group to accept denial of the problem and the discussion by individuals of their past life and problems. The latter may produce emotional arousal, so essential in changing attitudes. The group then offers a clear-cut solution to the member's problem, that is by giving up drinking. Finally there is the tremendous support available 24 hours a day between members. This is aided by the sponsorship system whereby an existing member who has been sober for a period supports ('sponsors') a new member.

Similarities between A. A. and religious sects have been noted (Jones, 1970). He points out that A. A. as a movement subscribes to a belief in some form of God although this is not specified. Indeed it is usually emphasized that by 'God' is meant 'a higher power greater than ourselves', which can be freely interpreted by different individuals. He describes A. A. as a means of providing conversion with a switching of attitudes including change from 'conscience-ridden' to 'conscience-free'. Out of a total of 50 respondent members of A. A. (total size of sample not stated) 44 spoke of conversion and felt A. A. offered a new way of life. Whether or not parallel can be drawn between A. A. and particular religious sects does not appear to the author of great importance. Clearly there are resemblances between A. A. and all types of groups (political, religious, therapeutic, etc.) which are concerned with changing attitude and behaviour. What requires further study is quantification of attitude change, an understanding of the manner in which this is done, and why some members change more than others. A. A. also fills another important function. For many alcoholics giving up alcohol means giving up a way of life often centred on the bar or public house. A. A. offers a means of filling that gap created by abstinence. Edwards *et al.* (1967a) have examined a sample of members attending A. A. groups in London. Males predominated in the sample, whose mean age was 45.7 years. The present social class distribution was I (upper) 9 per cent, II 26 per cent, III 50 per cent IV 10 per cent and V 4 per cent. The overall picture resembled that of patients attending alcoholism treatment units (Hore and Smith, 1975) and information centres (Edwards *et al.*, 1967b) in England and Wales and is clearly different from 'Skid Row' (Edwards *et al.*, 1966). Edwards *et al.* (1967a) in relation to A. A. concluded 'that 'A. A. selects—despite the declared policy of having no bar to membership, there are inevitable covert and dynamic selection processes at work. . . . Selection is not affected by showing the non-conforming member the door but by establishing norms of what the good A. A. member is to be.'

The comment is often made that the recovered alcoholic exchanges his dependency on alcohol for dependency on A. A. Indeed, in the study already mentioned (Gerard, Saenger and Wiley, 1962) this has been emphasized. Implied in this criticism is the philosophy that treatment of the alcoholic should enable him to give up his dependency totally. Whilst this would obviously be ideal, with present techniques it would appear realistic to accept that many alcoholics will require dependency on some agency for a prolonged period. Membership of A. A. is unlikely to do harm to the individual and his sobriety at least avoids the tremendous problems arising from alcohol misuse.

A. A. has two fellow organizations, Alanon and a more recent development, Aliteen. The first is designed to help the relatives of the alcoholic, the latter the children of the alcoholic. Both use the group meeting as their principal therapeutic tool.

SOCIAL SERVICES DEPARTMENTS

Apart from financial contributions to Councils of Alcoholism and other agencies, etc., Social Services Departments have recently begun to make important contributions to community management in Britain. These include the appointment of social workers specifically appointed to assist in developing services for alcoholics and the opening of treatment agencies under the auspices of the Department. In 1971 in Manchester such a social worker was appointed and in 1973 the Department established its own therapeutic hostel for alcoholics.

PROBATION SERVICE

In view of the close link between criminal behaviour and alcoholism the probation officer has an important diagnostic, counselling and link function (with other agencies); often, however, he is dealing with clients other agencies do not wish to meet, and perhaps it may be necessary for separate facilities to be set up, particularly for psychopathic clients.

OTHER AGENCIES

For many years religious organizations in particular, including the Salvation Army and Church Army, have attempted to help alcoholics, often dealing with alcoholics that nobody else wanted. This has been particularly true concerning the shelter needs of the alcoholic. Such valuable contributions will continue to be required although it is hoped that in developing programmes such service will be linked to others and not operate in isolation.

REFERENCES

Bristol Council of Alcoholism (1972). 2nd Annual Report. 14 Park Row, Bristol BS1 5LJ

Cook, T., Morgan, H. G. and Pollak, B. (1968). 'The Rathcoole experiment.' 'First year at a hostel for vagrant alcoholics.' *Br. med. J.* 1, 240

Coventry and Warwickshire Council of Alcoholism (1971). 2nd Annual Report. 5a Priory Row, Coventry CV1 5EX

Edwards, G., Hawker, A. and Hensman, C. (1966). 'Setting up a therapeutic community.' *Lancet* 2, 1407

Edwards, G., Williamson, V., Hawker, A. and Hensman, C. (1966). 'London's Skid Row.' *Lancet* 1, 249

Edwards, G., Hensman, C. Hawker, A. and Williamson, V. (1967a). 'Alcoholics Anonymous: the anatomy of a self help group.' *Soc. Psychiat.* 1, 195

Edwards, G., Fisher, M. K., Hawker, A. and Hensman, C. (1967b). 'Clients of Alcoholism Information Centres.' *Br. med. J.* 4, 346

Gerard, D. L., Saenger G. and Wiley R. (1962). 'The abstinent alcoholic.' *Archs gen. Psychiat.* 6, 83

Helping Hand Organisation (1972). Annual Report. 8 Strutton Ground, London SW1

Hore, B. D. and Smith, E. (1975). 'Who goes to alcoholism treatment units.' *Br. J. Addict.* 70, 263

Ingram-Smith, N. (1967). 'Alcoholic Rehabilitation Centre of the West London Mission.' *Br. J. Addict.* 62, 295

Jones, K. (1970). 'Alcoholics Anonymous–a new revivalism.' *New Society* 16 July 1970, p. 102

Kenyon W. (1974). 'The co-ordination and interaction of treatment and rehabilitation facilities for alcoholism in the Merseyside region.' *Proceedings Alcoholism Manchester, June 1974* International Council on Alcohol and Addiction, Lausanne

Merseyside Council of Alcoholism (1970). Report. Merseyside Council Chambers B15, The Temple, Dale St, Liverpool L2 5RU

Myerson, D. J. and Mayer J. (1966). 'Origins, treatment and destiny of Skid Row alcoholic men.' *New Engl. J. Med.* **275,** 419

15

DEVELOPING A COMMUNITY SERVICE

Alcoholism treatment services have developed in an *ad hoc* way from a variety of both statutory and voluntary agencies. Such development often produces at least overlapping of functions and often frank rivalry with the conviction held that there is only one way, that of a particular agency, to help the alcoholic.

The logical development of services would begin with an indication of the size of the problem in any community and the type of clients already known to existing agencies. As regards the former, as outlined previously, prevalence studies have been either indirect or direct. Indirect studies are usually of two types: firstly, the use of Jellinek formula (W. H. O., 1951) or other indirect indices, and secondly, asking existing treatment agencies how many alcoholics they know to exist in a particular community (e.g. Parr, 1954; Moss and Davies, 1967). Direct studies involve either the use of community surveys (e.g. Bailey, Haberman and Alksne, 1965) or direct questionnaire studies of an 'at risk population' (e.g. Wilkins, 1974).

The Jellinek formula, although much criticized (Popham 1956; Seeley, 1959), has been found to compare favourably with direct studies, as outlined in Chapter 7.

Direct studies for obvious reasons been confined either to particular areas in the country or to a particular population, and may not be applicable to other populations, let alone other areas. Obtaining some idea of the size of the problem in a particular area or community should enable one to obtain some insight into the need for extending facilities. In a study in south London, Edwards *et al.* (1973) found that the number of clients with drinking problems was one ninth to one quarter of those known to agencies. In Manchester using much cruder data (Hore, 1973) it would appear existing facilities are coping with a

144

small fraction of clients believed to exist within the city, with the clear majority of clients not receiving help. Even if, as is certainly true, not all patients with drinking problems are prepared to seek help it indicates the size of the problem and encourages one to seek new ways of reaching the 'submerged' majority.

Further, it is important to see which facilities are being most used. Thus in Manchester there are only two facilities dealing with large numbers, these being Alcoholics Anonymous and the Alcoholism Treatment Unit (Hore, 1973).

In any community with existing services it is vital to know the characteristics of clients attending these agencies. Are the services predominantly helping the socially stable alcoholics or are they orientated towards 'Skid Row'? Although studies have been carried out (Edwards *et al.*, 1967a, b; Hore and Smith, 1975) of the types of clients attending A. A., information centres and alcoholism treatment units respectively, there have been few national studies or studies confined to several areas. Again, in any particular community it is logical that careful recording be made of the types of clients attending such agencies. Such data should be standardized so each agency can be compared.

Hore and Smith (1975) showed that the client population of alcoholic units ranges from high to low social stability in units situated in different parts of the country. It would seem likely however that in most cities only a minority of clients are receiving attention. Whilst failure to attract clients may be due to the incorrect type of facilities offered and there is clearly a need for identification of submerged clients and for experimentation, it has to be emphasized that many clients with drinking problems, even if identified successfully, are unwilling to accept the need for help. Such help may be acceptable only if pressure is applied by relatives, employers, etc. In relation to the latter as described previously, Britain stands out unfavourably compared with the U. S. A. Major companies in the U. S. A. have developed alcoholism programmes in which pressure can be applied to an alcoholic without him necessarily losing his job. The lack of such programmes in British industry stands in glaring contrast.

At this stage it may be useful to look at the type of facilities offered at present and differing types of function. As stated previously, hospital in-patient facilities are probably indicated only for a minority of alcoholics apart from patients suffering from diseases associated with heavy drinking, such as cirrhosis of the liver or peripheral neuropathy. Admission to hospital would appear to have the following functions: firstly, detoxification; secondly, to provide a secure alcohol-free environment in which a drinking bout can be interrupted; thirdly, as a place where specialized techniques such as group therapy and aversion therapy can be practised. Alcoholism treatment centres act as a 'referral sink' (in Manchester the annual referral rate has risen from 300 p.a. to 500 p.a. over the last two years), a specialized treatment agency and a research centre. Although detoxification centres have existed outside hospitals it would seem preferable for such facilities to be inside hospitals in view of the potential seriousness of the withdrawal syndrome (albeit rare). 'Shelters' other than a hospital could be thought of but they would have to be secure. Specialized techniques such as group therapy and aversion therapy could be given outside a hospital, but resources rarely enable this to happen to the same degree of intensity outside a hospital.

Alcoholics Anonymous appears to deal with the more socially stable clients as do information centres. There would appear no doubt that A. A. works for many but it is also well known not all clients are prepared to attend regularly and enter the programme. Other types of community-based non-institutional group programmes apart from A. A. are required. Work currently being carried out in Liverpool using outpatient Education group counselling sessions under the Merseyside Council of Alcoholism (Kenyon, personal communication, 1974) shows encouraging results. Information centres as run by Councils of Alcoholism appear to pick up a similar type of client but perhaps at an earlier stage. The quantitative contribution they make in three cities has already been described in the previous chapter. Hostels, as outlined previously, provide an environment promoting sobriety but in the community. More general hostels such as those provided by the Salvation Army, Church Army, etc. may have primarily an identification function, as clearly do the probation and prison services.

Although functions of these agencies will overlap, they may all be essential in a particular community with differing emphasis according to the needs of that community. The most vital thing is that they work as an integrated whole, aware of the value of other contributions. This will not happen and entrenched positions will be taken up unless firstly there is an acceptance of other people's role, and secondly there is regular contact and frank discussion between the agencies. Such contact will perhaps enable expansion of existing individual agencies to go ahead in the light of local needs. In Manchester for the last three years there have been regular (at least monthly) meetings between the agencies where frank discussion has taken place of different types of services. Such a group can generate its own strength and attempt to work towards a unified solution. This three year's work has culminated in the setting up of a Greater Manchester Council of Alcoholism, whilst previous attempts in the last decade without this groundwork being done have failed. Disagreements between members of the group have been frequent but there has been the opportunity to voice them openly and a serious attempt made to avoid entrenched positions. Development of a comprehensive community service would appear to involve the following steps:

1. Knowledge of the size of the problem in a particular area.
2. Knowledge of the types of clients who are and who are not being attracted into the existing agencies, with consequent improvement of existing agencies, and the development of further agencies to increase identification and offer treatment.
3. Clarification of the essential functions of differing agencies and clients and staff expectations of these agencies.
4. Positive attempts made to provide regular contact between all the agencies involved.
5. Futher development of individual services in the light of the different needs and regular re-evaluation of effectiveness of the agencies.

REFERENCES

Bailey, M., Haberman, P. and Alksne, H. (1965). 'The epidemiology of alcoholism in an urban residential area.' *Q. Jl Stud. Alcohol* **26**, 19

Edwards, G., Hensman, C., Hawker, A. and Williamson, V. (1967a). 'Alcoholics Anonymous: the anatomy of a self help group.' *Soc. Psychiat.* **1**, 195

Edwards, G., Fisher, M. K., Hawker, A. and Hensman, C. (1967b). 'Clients of Alcoholism Information Centres.' *Br. med. J.* **4**, 346

Edwards, G., Hawker, A., Hensman, C., Peto, J. and Williamson, V. (1973). 'Alcoholics known or unknown to agencies–epidemiological studies in a London suburb.' *Br. J. Psychiat.* **123**, 169

Hore, B. D. (1973). 'Development of a community-orientated treatment programme for alcoholics.' In *Alcoholism–A Medical Profile. Proceedings 1st International Medical Conference on Alcoholism London, 1973*. Ed. by N. Kessel, A. Hawker and H. Chalke, London; B. Edsall

Hore, B. D. and Smith, E. (1975). 'Who goes to alcoholic units.' *Br. J. Addict.* **70**, 263

Moss, M. C. and Davies, E. B. (1967). 'A survey of alcoholism in an English county.' London; Geigy Scientific Publications

Parr, D. (1954). 'Alcoholism in general practice.' *Br. J. Addict.* **54**, 25

Popham, R. (1956). 'The Jellinek alcoholism estimation formula and its application to Canadian data.' *Q. Jl Stud. Alcohol* **17**, 559

Seeley, J. (1959). 'Estimating the prevalence of alcoholism–a critical analysis of the Jellinek formula.' *Q. Jl Stud. Alcohol* **20**, 245

W. H. O. (1951). *Tech. Rep. Ser. Wld Hlth Org.* No. 142

Wilkins, R. H. (1974). 'The hidden alcoholic in general practice.' London; Elek Science

INDEX